WRIGHTSVILLE BEACH

Also by Ray McAllister

WRIGHTSVILLE BEACH
The Luminous Island

Ray McAllister

JOHN F. BLAIR
PUBLISHER
Winston-Salem, North Carolina

The paper in this book meets the guidelines for permanence and durability of the Committee on Production Guidelines for Book Longevity of the Council on Library Resources.

First Printing 2007

Printed in North Carolina

Design and composition by Angela Harwood

Library of Congress Cataloging-in-Publication Data

McAllister, Ray, 1952-
  Wrightsville Beach: The Luminous Island / Ray McAllister.
      p. cm.
  Includes bibliographical references and index.
  ISBN-13: 978-0-89587-347-7 (hardcover : alk. paper)
  ISBN-10: 0-89587-347-8 (hardcover : alk. paper)
  ISBN-13: 978-0-89587-348-4 (pbk. : alk. paper)
  ISBN-10: 0-89587-348-6 (pbk. : alk. paper) 1. Wrightsville Beach (N.C.)--History. 2.   Wrightsville Beach (N.C.)--History--Pictorial works. 3. Wrightsville Beach Region (N.C.)--History. 4. Wrightsville Beach Region (N.C.)--History--Pictorial works. I. Title.

  F264.W9M38 2007
  975.6'27--dc22

                              2007015632

For Lindsay, Micah, and Riley

Contents

Preface

Writing one book inevitably leads to a "What's next?" When the first book is personal, though, as mine about Topsail Island was, the question becomes almost problematic. I long had been drawn to the North Carolina coast. But Topsail was our family's out-of-the-way favorite. Would any other subject have quite the connection?

The answer, it turned out, was beneath our feet. Vicki and I had visited Wrightsville Beach through the years, taking side trips with our children whenever we visited my parents in Wilmington. The beach was only 10 minutes away. We would take Lindsay, Ryan, and Jamie down for a couple of hours of sea and sand during the summer. Other seasons, it might be a walk along the surf's edge or out onto Johnnie Mercer's Fishing Pier. Even now, one of our favorite stops on these visits is the Oceanic Restaurant, overlooking the surf. We could stay there for hours, were it not for waiting diners.

Nature got the Carolina coast right. And part of what is inviting about Wrightsville is that man hasn't fully undone nature's work. Not yet, anyway. Even when we began visiting, beach cottages seemed to fill every available stretch of sand, and, yes, there were large hotels and small shops. It would be hard to maintain that Wrightsville is "undiscovered." But whether by design, luck, or a combination, the island seems to have kept away the more grotesque signs of commerce that foul other large resorts. Wrightsville is a beach town that hasn't yet overpowered the beach.

It was my editor at John F. Blair, Publisher—Steve Kirk—who suggested there was a book here. The island has a good bit of history, he said. He said it almost offhandedly, as if aware of what I would find.

Call it an understatement. Like most of North Carolina's barrier islands, Wrightsville has rich tales of pirates, Native Americans, settlers, fishermen, hurricanes, and even fires. But there is much more here. The island's first structure was a yacht club, put up more than a century and a half ago on a deserted, wind-swept strand. Moreover, for more than a century now, Wrightsville has been a desired spot for vacationers. "The Playground of the South," it was called. Few resorts have had this kind of history.

And if you've never heard of Lumina . . . well, suffice to say for now, Lumina lit up the island. Figuratively. Literally. They don't make them like that anymore. They did only once.

It became a pleasure piecing together the story of Wrightsville, tearing into old newspaper articles, scouring museums and libraries, talking with islanders and vacationers. Just walking the beach. Soon, history was riding in on the waves. Forgotten landmarks, now mere curiosities to vacationers, began to call up their stories.

The book that has emerged is a walk down the beach of today, kicking at the sand, looking for those old stories that lie just below, like seashells or sharks' teeth.

A word about nomenclature: The names Wrightsville Beach and Wrightsville are used interchangeably here. Historically, that is wrong: Wrightsville was the village on the mainland alongside Wrightsville Sound whose development preceded that of the Wrightsville Beach barrier island. But this is a book of the 21st century, when the old village has been swallowed up by the Wilmington area and the names are used colloquially as synonyms. Similarly, where there are historical disputes, this book goes with the most likely version or, if none has an advantage, presents them all. The same applies to disputed names. The famed hotels are the Seashore and the Tarrymoore here, though they are called the Sea Shore and the Tarrymore in some old accounts. Hugh MacRae's island development enterprise is Tide Water Power Company, though it is often referred to elsewhere as the Tidewater Power Company.

One last thing. This book is intended as an entertaining read more than a formal history lesson. It does admit to an agenda, however: If you don't find within these pages encouragement for preserving not only the history but the *character* of this island and others like it, then it has failed. Likely, though, you already feel that Wrightsville is a place, a feeling, a *heritage* worth embracing and handing down to ensuing generations.

If you don't, you soon will.

What a story this old beach town has!

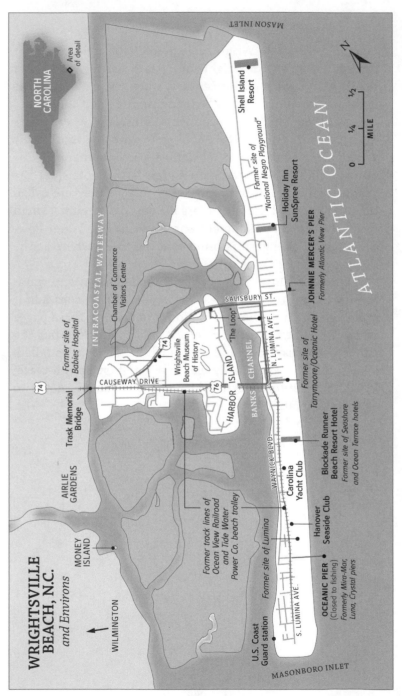

WRIGHTSVILLE BEACH, N.C.
and Environs

NORTH CAROLINA

Area of detail

WILMINGTON

MONEY ISLAND

AIRLIE GARDENS

Former site of Babies Hospital

INTRACOASTAL WATERWAY

Chamber of Commerce Visitors Center

Trask Memorial Bridge

CAUSEWAY DRIVE

Wrightsville Beach Museum of History

SALISBURY ST.

"The Loop"

HARBOR ISLAND

BANKS CHANNEL

Former track lines of Ocean View Railroad and Tide Water Power Co. beach trolley

Former site of Lumina

Carolina Yacht Club

Hanover Seaside Club

WARWICK BLVD.

Blockade Runner Beach Resort Hotel
Former site of Seashore and Ocean Terrace hotels

N. LUMINA AVE.

Former site of Tarrymoore/Oceanic Hotel

JOHNNIE MERCER'S PIER
Formerly Atlantic View Pier

Holiday Inn SunSpree Resort

Former site of "National Negro Playground"

Shell Island Resort

MASON INLET

ATLANTIC OCEAN

U.S. Coast Guard station

OCEANIC PIER
(Closed to fishing)
Formerly Mira-Mar, Luna, Crystal piers

S. LUMINA AVE.

MASONBORO INLET

0   ¼   ½   MILE

N

MAP BY ROY WILHELM

Chapter One

THE LUMINOUS ISLAND

Mornings are made for the beach.

It is winter now, the summer crowds a memory, but the day is warm enough that the memory is easily recalled. The sands of Wrightsville Beach are almost deserted before sunrise. There are no signs—save the two piers reaching into the ocean—that anyone has been here in a thousand years.

Soon, a couple comes walking by, here to see the sunrise, the day's first venturers onto this section of beach. A man in a green jacket appears with a camera. A woman in a red bathrobe walks out onto the Silver Gull Motel's balcony above, leaning against the rail as she looks outward.

No one is in any particular hurry.

If the sun wants to take its time, so will they.

The sun is just beginning to make its appearance. The advance guard, brilliant sky-filling rays of orange, trumpets the arrival. A sliver of moon tries to hang onto the sky that it will soon relinquish.

Overhead, a flock of 30 birds flies in tight formation. Not to be outdone, sea gulls stop picking at the surf and take to the air. Theirs is a unit of about 30 as well, but disorganized, out of formation. They appear ungainly as a group.

An early-morning beach walker takes a sunrise stroll, with dog in front and infant son on his back. The lights on Johnnie Mercer's Pier are still on. Minutes from now they will be overpowered by the sun.
PHOTO BY VICKI McALLISTER

Individually, though, they glide beautifully, gracefully on the breeze. They are artists of the air, not formation pilots.

A dozen or more people are here for the sky show unfolding now. A couple sits wrapped in a blanket. Others walk. Some stand.

Down the beach, one man has set up a tripod and camera. Jonathan Guetta is an environmental consultant from Wilmington. But it is his avocation, amateur astronomy, that has brought him here so early. He is seeking not the perfect sunrise picture but a comet, no easy quest. Guetta's astronomy club has learned the days are running out. The comet still appears low on the horizon near sunrise and sunset, but soon it will sink too low.

Guetta's attempt this morning ends in failure. The comet is blocked by either banks of clouds or the brilliant sun.

No matter. "It's nice being here anyway," he says before giving up. "No harm in not seeing it." He smiles. He will wait just a little longer.

The sun is now above the horizon, its luminescent glow overpowering the thin early-morning clouds and glistening off the white-capped waves. The water lights up. Soon, the island will, too, and it will remain so until evening, when the sun will depart just a few hundred yards to the west, sinking into the channel in an explosion of reds and oranges. Long before famed Lumina lit up the coastline, Wrightsville was awash in color.

The couple wrapped in the blanket has gotten up and moved on, walking up the beach, one supposes, or retreating to breakfast now that the light show is done. Runners have appeared. So have more walkers, as well as seekers of small treasures. They scan the sand in front of them, then the ocean, then the sand, then the ocean.

Beach walks, especially in the mornings when one's own footprints are the first, renourish the soul. Wrightsville has its share of beach walkers—more than its share, thanks to the absence of gaudy commercialism. They walk in the surf, pick for shells, talk together. They spend time with the ocean and with themselves.

Megan Walter is a morning beach runner. She glides just above the surf line, where the sand is smoothest and packed hardest, doing seven to nine miles a day, four days a week. "I love it," she says of this place, stopping momentarily. "It's very peaceful. It relieves a lot of stress." She has to be at work by nine at a real-estate firm, where she is a marketing coordinator. This is her time.

Nature provides Walter moments of magic. The sunrise, of course. Sometimes, sand dollars deposited by the nighttime tide. "The other day, I saw dolphins jumping out of the water," she adds, "jumping straight up." Walter has been running the beach for four years, since moving down from Apex, near the center of the state. She doesn't want to go back.

There is human magic as well. "I've seen a couple people get engaged. I saw someone propose under the pier," Walter says, gesturing behind her, "and another one up there on the sand." One can't beat that: new lives together, starting at sunrise by the ocean.

Tom Bragan, who visits four times a year from Arlington, Virginia, carries his nine-month-old son on his back. Both are pulled along at breakneck speed by their large Labrador retriever, Mookie.

But Brian Bailey walks the beach at the pace of his soon-to-be-four-year-old daughter, Amelia. That is to say enthusiastically, haltingly, seemingly without design. Amelia splashes in the surf, comes out, goes in, comes out, walks up to a sea gull.

Bailey has been coming here for about 15 years, going back to the days when he was a teenager living with his family in Maryland. He remembers staying at the Holiday Inn SunSpree when ocean waters would come right up to, and under, the hotel. Bailey lives now in Hillsborough, North Carolina, where he is a culinary teacher at a community college. He and his wife usually stay at the relocated SunSpree or the Blockade Runner. But their trips to Wrightsville are seasonal, more often in winter than other times. Wrightsville is simply too crowded in summer. The Baileys visit Topsail Island instead.

He and Amelia are walking the beach this morning ostensibly looking for sharks' teeth, seashells, and ocean glass. Amelia seems to have other plans. "She loves it. She loves to be here, though the water's cold," Bailey says. "She'll walk in, see it's cold, and walk out, then walk in again. She likes the sea gulls." While Dad is talking, little Amelia is engaged in conversation, too, with a sea gull. The gull, disinterested, walks away. Amelia continues talking.

Just a few feet up the beach, Josh Winneberger stands behind a camera on a tripod aimed at a half-dozen early-morning surfers. The camera is a Canon Rebel XTI with a 300-meter zoom lens, and Winneberger has been hired by two friends to take surfing shots of them.

Winneberger, a high-school student, is a surfer himself and speaks up for Wrightsville Beach. "It's actually one of the better places on the East Coast for surfing," he says. It obviously doesn't have the large waves of Florida or New Jersey or North Carolina's Outer Banks. But the waves are better than one would expect. "I guess it's all the sand bars," he explains.

There's something about this magical bit of coastline. Everyone finds something. Indians, pirates, and blockade runners once worked it of necessity. Boaters, fishermen, swimmers, and divers followed by choice. And surfers. Families have played here on the beach for well over a century, brought first by trains, then beach trolleys, now cars. Dancers,

The morning pace is set by a young girl, not quite four years old. She goes in and out of the surf, taking her time, as if there is all the time in the world. Early mornings on Wrightsville Beach are like that.
PHOTOGRAPH BY VICKI McALLISTER

diners, revelers, and even movie watchers have looked out over the seas.

Wrightsville has gone from a lonely outpost to an island of small summer cottages to a paradise for real-estate investors. The island has been battered by ungodly storms, unholy fires, and undeterred developers. Only the surf and the shifting sands of the beach have survived them all.

No one needs the beach more this morning than Lynn Taylor.

She is carrying a bag of beach finds—"beautiful shells," she says easily, "to capture the memory of my time down here." She needs a positive memory. Her mother died before Christmas. Now, her father has gone into the hospital with renal failure. She is from Lexington, North Carolina, where she helped found a statewide homeschooling organization, but she had been staying with her parents in South Carolina. A friend has let Taylor use her beach condo this weekend. She needs Wrightsville Beach. She needs this time.

"This is part of life," Taylor says philosophically. "A time to reflect. I woke up about 2:30 this morning and just went out on the balcony and watched the stars." She never did go back to sleep. Her eyes now are both tired and sad. But she seems at least momentarily at peace. The beach reassures her, she says, that "the flow of life goes on."

She reaches into the bag and pulls out something. It does not appear to be a shell but an oblong rock, brown and worn smooth, intriguing in its shape and its unknown origin. She picked it up as a conversation piece. "It makes you think of pirates and treasure," she offers.

She looks up, seemingly unsure as to whether or not it makes one think of that at all. She smiles, then continues walking the beach.

Chapter Two

THE PIRATES AND MONEY ISLAND

In the late fall of 1858, a small schooner appeared off the coast of what is now Wrightsville Beach, sailing along the shore for a mile or two, then retracing the route. Occasionally, it stopped for a short time, as if searching for an exact location. Just before sunset, the schooner sailed through Masonboro Inlet and dropped its hooks into Banks Channel, behind the island.

An old man sitting in his skiff and tonging oysters in the salt marsh watched silently. In the full moon, he saw a small boat let down over the side. Several figures got in. They began rowing toward a tiny, deserted island in the mouth of Bradley Creek.

The man, described in the *Wilmington Herald* as an "old negro," saw lights darting among the oaks and cedars that populated the one-acre island. Dark forms moved, too, as if they were searching. After perhaps an hour, the lanterns were doused. The men returned to the boat, threaded their way back to the ship, boarded, and left. What they had wanted—what they had done—was unclear.

The next day, the old man returned to the island.

Under one of the largest trees, he found a huge hole, freshly dug. Next to it was a corresponding mound of dirt. Along the sides of the hole were tracks of rust. They appeared to be the same distance apart as the iron bands on a large chest.

Who the hunters were was never determined. Neither was what they found. But excitement grew after a newspaper story appeared. The public had a fair idea of what they were after, and the island was quickly named Money Island. It was not long before other treasure seekers began swarming Money Island. Soon, it was dotted with holes whose diggers apparently came away empty.

Legend has it that more than one pirate buried his booty on the island, which is far smaller today but can still be seen from various locations, including the bridge to Wrightsville Beach a mile north and Airlie Gardens on the mainland. Jack Ketch was one such pirate. Captain Redfield was another. Possibly even the notorious Blackbeard, one of many pirates who worked the North Carolina coast at that time. Others included Stede Bonnet, Charles Vane, Christopher Moody, William Lewis, and William Fly.

The Money Island legend has a firm rationale. Burying treasure along the shifting outer islands might mean it would be lost forever. But a pirate who buried it on an inner island could mark and return to the spot—unless he was killed first.

One Money Island story has persisted: The treasure is Captain Kidd's.

William Kidd, born in 1645, was a British privateer commissioned in 1695 to apprehend pirates. But by 1697, he turned pirate himself, taking several ships and killing his own gunner. Eventually, Kidd surrendered, denying his piracy and believing he had been promised a pardon. He was returned to England, where he was tried instead and hanged in 1701. Some of his treasure, used at trial, had been dug up off Long Island, New York.

But much apparently was never found.

Enter Andrew J. Howell, Jr., a Wilmington writer, historian, and Presbyterian minister who told the story of Kidd in his 1908 book, *Money Island*. Howell's parents had owned a summer home nearby. As a boy, he was sometimes free to roam the waters, beaches, and islands. While he and a friend were sailing one summer night, they came upon a boat on the south side of Money Island. They waited an hour or so on the beach, then brought their boat close enough to see two men sitting by a campfire in front of a tent. Excitement overtook the boys.

Howell wrote, "I had heard from my early childhood that Captain Kidd, the historic and lordly pirate, who reigned supreme upon the high seas during the seventeenth century, was supposed to have buried some of his booty on Money Island. Everybody was familiar with the tradition; and I doubt if there is, even now, a single person reared in the town of Wilmington, or in the vicinity of the Sound, who has not likewise been told the same indefinite story about the little island. But the presence of these two strangers, and their somewhat mysterious conduct, give a tradition a touch of reality such as it could never have otherwise had."

The boys decided to come back the following morning as if they had just happened upon the island. One of the men appeared to be more than 60 years old and said his name was Jonathan Landstone. He and his partner believed the treasure was there. They had been digging for four days, though. That meant that either the island had shifted and the treasure was now underwater or that it was embedded beneath the massive roots of two oak trees.

Money Island, shown here in the early 20th century, lies between Wrightsville Beach and the mainland. Once a tree-filled acre, the island has succumbed to nearby dredging projects, wave-making boats, and other ravages of time. It is now little more than a spit of sand in the Intracoastal Waterway.

NEW HANOVER PUBLIC LIBRARY, LOUIS T. MOORE COLLECTION

At supper that evening, Landstone, after prodding, agreed to share his facts if the boys kept them secret.

Landstone, who lived in Philadelphia, said he had heard the story years earlier from his grandfather. That grandfather, who had made two unsuccessful attempts to find the treasure, had in turn heard the story from his father late in the latter's life. His father was the pirate John Redfield.

Captain John Redfield was Kidd's trusted counselor. One morning after a successful voyage, Kidd sailed his ship to near the spot where Howell and the others now sat. He directed Redfield to help him bury his treasure, to make the area his home as Kidd sailed on, and to take $1,000 for expenses.

Kidd added, "You are to keep the engagement, if necessary, for five years. Our calling, as you know, is a little uncertain. At the end of that period, if I have not returned, you will be at liberty to take up the smaller chest to be deposited to-night, and use the contents, subject to such division—not to exceed one-half to each of us—as I may demand on my return. The same conditions will apply to the other chest for an additional period of five years."

Kidd, Redfield, and four other pirates dug two holes

10 feet apart, buried the chests, and replanted a small tree above each. Kidd and the four pirates went back to the ship, then sailed off with the crew.

Kidd, it turned out, was executed in London not long after.

Redfield, meanwhile, had been left with four men who knew nothing of the treasure. He lived on the mainland nearby. He traveled occasionally to the new colony of Charleston and brought home a wife.

Some 19 months after Kidd's departure, a boat arrived, headed by another of his pirates, Max Brisbau. He claimed Kidd wanted the chests, though he did not have Kidd's seal as evidence. He and Redfield began fighting. With the help of his wife, Redfield tied up Brisbau. An hour later, Brisbau's men returned with Redfield's. All now knew of the treasure. When Redfield refused to say where it was buried, he and his wife were held in chains.

Brisbau and his crew set off for Charleston, promising to return and kill Redfield if he did not have a change of heart. Brisbau and his men, however, were imprisoned in Charleston for piracy. Redfield and his wife finally moved away, never digging up the treasure.

Redfield's son, after hearing the story near the end of his father's life, made two unsuccessful attempts to find Captain Kidd's treasure.

And now here was Redfield's great-grandson Jonathan Landstone attempting to dig it up.

"Mr. Landstone, do you really believe that story?" Howell asked.

Landstone laughed and said, "Well, you see, I am on an undertaking I have had in mind for nearly fifty years. Yes, I believe those chests are there."

The two men and two boys got digging in the morning. It took all day to pull up one massively rooted tree. Water began filling the hole, but not before they struck something hard. Howell took off his clothes and jumped in. With a shovel, he brought up a piece of rusty sheet iron. Running their hands through the sand from the hole, each member of the group found several coins. The silver ones were mostly corroded, but the gold coins were intact.

"We concluded that the remaining chest had probably been removed," Howell wrote, "but that is still an unsettled question."

Howell's is an intriguing story, even if the numbers don't add up. He wrote that he first heard the tale "when I was a boy in the early forties." He had spoken little of it since. "In my old age, however, I am going to let my tale forsake its hiding place and become public property."

In other words, Howell contended he heard the story from Landstone in the '40s—the 1840s—though Howell was not born until 1869. As for telling the story in his "old age," the book was published when he was 39.

Howell's story seems more a good novel. Indeed, Bland Simpson, writing in *The Inner Islands,* said Howell's estate offered the story to the RKO Motion Picture Company in the 1940s. RKO's representative wrote back, "I have read *Money Island* with considerable interest. It is a fine yarn, but is nothing I can make into a picture at the present time."

The story remains alluring.

Historians say Captain Kidd did sail past the North Carolina coast. In fact, Kidd did bury treasure—in the Long Island area. There are legends of his burying portions elsewhere, including in the Connecticut River of Massachusetts. An Internet search also turns up stories of Kidd burying his treasure on Money Island—but on a Money Island in New

Jersey, or near a Money Island in Connecticut.

Treasure hunters have continued searching the Money Island that is Wrightsville Beach's neighbor.

It was not until 1939, some 81 years after the small schooner made its nighttime stop reported in the old *Wilmington Herald*, that a second find was made on the island—or a third, if you count Howell's. Two boys from Wilmington, O. E. Parker and W. S. Northrop, were exploring the island for scrap iron. They found a large iron chest banded with studded iron strips and protected by a massive locking apparatus with a keyhole. The chest was badly corroded, and its oak plank interior had rotted away. It was also, the boys told a newspaper reporter, empty.

The most persistent of legends has it that Captain William Kidd, known to have buried treasure elsewhere, buried some on Money Island as well. He was hanged in 1701 before he could return. Numerous holes have been dug by those trying to find it. Have they?

ILLUSTRATION BY HOWARD PYLE, FIRST APPEARANCE IN *HARPER'S NEW MONTHLY MAGAZINE*, DECEMBER 1902

Imaginations, however, are not empty. The lure of finding pirate treasure on Money Island persists. The evidence is at best inconclusive. But to treasure hunters or the merely romantic, two pieces of circumstantial evidence are worth noting.

Treasure may well have been buried right here on Money Island.

And it may never have been found.

Chapter Three

THE MYSTERY OF THE BLOCKADE RUNNER

On Friday morning, February 19, 1864, the *Richmond Dispatch* had disheartening news for the leaders of the Confederate government and other readers in the capital city:

Loss of the *Scotia*

The loss of the steamer *Scotia* (the *Fannie and Jennie*), off the North Carolina coast, has been noticed. She was chased by the blockader *Georgia* and run on the beach on Wrightsville Sound. The boats of the blockader then made for her, and the crew of the *Scotia* started to take to her boats. While one of these, containing the Captain, Purser, and others was being lowered, the davit broke, spilling them all into the sea. Some of these were rescued, in a sinking and exhausted condition by the second and third mates in the other starboard boat, while others got ashore by clinging to trunks and other articles thrown overboard from the steamer. Wm. F. Jones, chief engineer, Wm. Morrel, his

1st assistant, and E. J. Black quartermaster, were drowned. The following of the crew are missing: G. H. Tailour, Geo. Davis, H. Thompson, John Steward, Wm. Burke, Grieson, Purcell, Duffy, Buchanan, Collins, Hughes, Hall, Clos, Shearn, Kempton, Lynch, Greaser, Barlow, Holtidge, Smith, and Wallace. Chas. Lightfoot, the confused cabin boy, was drowned.

Details in that early newspaper account would prove not entirely accurate. The *Fanny and Jenny* was confused with the British steamer *Scotia*—with an odd reference to *Fannie and Jennie* only raising more questions—and the Union ship *Florida* with the *Georgia*. But the result was right. The *Fanny and Jenny* had gone down.

And with it went one of the mysteries of the Civil War, unsolved to this day.

Soon after the Civil War began in April 1861, President Abraham Lincoln declared a commercial and military blockade of Southern ports. Among the most important was Wilmington. Within months, the Union had 75 vessels along the Carolina coast, then the largest American fleet ever assembled, to deprive the South of food, military hardware, and other supplies.

For most of the war, the blockaders and the smaller blockade runners engaged in a deadly game of cat and mouse. Most early blockade runners were sailing vessels. But their success was limited, so steamships—especially fast, shallow-draft side-wheel steamers—assumed the role. They were not cheap. The average steamer cost $150,000 in gold. But they were essential to the Confederate cause.

One such side-wheeler was the *Fanny and Jenny*. Some early accounts use the spellings *Fannie* or *Jennie*, but the Union commander's report and most later accounts use *Fanny and Jenny*. It was a valuable steamship, capable of a better-than-average speed of 14 knots an hour.

James Sprunt told the story of its demise in *Derelicts: An account of ships lost at sea in general commerce and a brief history of blockade runners stranded along the North Carolina coast, 1861–1865*. Sprunt was a philanthropist, a historian, and the owner of nearby Orton Plantation. He kept a summer home on Wrightsville Beach. As a teen nearly six decades earlier, he had served aboard a blockade runner in the Civil War. Now, in his 1920 book, Sprunt wrote of the *Fanny and Jenny*, which left Nassau in the Bahamas on February 4, 1864, and landed north of Wrightsville Beach on February 9:

> Her pilot, Burris, was not sure of his position, so he anchored the ship and made a landing in the surf to ascertain his bearings. It having been the intention of the captain to make land about two miles north of Fort Fisher, he then proceeded down the beach in the darkness. Unhappily, however, she stood too close in shore, and grounded repeatedly, and at about midnight stranded on a shoal a mile or two to the southward of where Lumina now stands. Early the next morning, the *Florida*, commanded by Captain Peirce Crosby, found her.
>
> Captain Crosby, desiring to save the *Fannie and Jennie* and realize big prize money, ran a hawser from his ship to the stranded vessel, intending to pull her off into deep water, when a Confederate flying battery of Whitworth guns of long range, from Fort Fisher, opened fire from Masonboro Beach, and with great precision cut off one of the

Florida's paddle-wheel arms, broke a second one, and cut a rim of the wheel in two; also, one of the Confederate shells exploded on board the *Florida* and came near destroying her. The *Florida* returned the fire, which so alarmed the captain and crew of the *Fannie and Jennie* that some of them attempted to reach the beach in boats. In this attempt Captain Coxetter and his purser were drowned in the breakers, the others gaining the shore; the rest of the crew, twenty-five in number, who remained on board were made prisoners by the Federals.

John Harden told a perhaps fanciful version of the story in his 1949 book, *The Devil's Tramping Ground and Other North Carolina Mystery Stories*. His version attached some literary meat to the historical bones of the story, and had the *Fanny and Jenny* ignoring the command to "heave to," instead opting to try to outrun the Federal blockader. A warning shot was fired, Harden wrote. Suddenly, another Union blockader fired a warning shot as well. When the blockade runner kept fleeing, the Union ships fired upon it. The *Fanny and Jenny* was hit repeatedly and began taking on water. The engines faltered. Union cannons continued firing. Harden wrote, "The beach was just ahead. All surviving hands rushed to the boats. The enemy, because of shoal water, fired a final volley and then dropped back to watch. The once sleek Clyde-built runner, her hold full of water, her cargo ruined, and her entire structure blasted by the enemy cannon fire, bumped along the ocean bottom, slumped over on her side, swung half-way around, and slowly sank to a final rest in the surf."

In reality, two blockade runners were involved with one Union ship, and not the other way around. The *Florida* tried to retrieve not only the *Fanny and Jenny* but also another grounded blockade runner, the *Emily of London*, whose captain and crew had left. But shelling from the Confederates at Fort Fisher forced the *Florida* to sink the *Emily* as well. Sprunt wrote, "She was then set on fire by bombshells from the cruiser *Florida*, a loud explosion on board of the wrecked vessel indicating that her cargo was probably partly composed of explosives for the Confederacy."

In his official report, filed the next day, Crosby said the captain and paymaster of the *Fanny and Jenny* drowned while trying to reach shore, while the 25 remaining crew members were captured. The *Fanny and Jenny*, he wrote, "was loaded with a few small articles of merchandise; had a good deal of coal." The captain added, "I have a Confederate flag, taken from the *Fanny and Jenny*, a spyglass, the chronometer, one sextant, and her charts."

Sunken blockade runners could be seen in the surf for generations after the war, as they went down in shallow water and were built mostly of thick iron that didn't corrode easily. Sprunt wrote, "For many years, the summer visitors on Wrightsville Beach have looked out upon the hurrying swell of the broad Atlantic and have felt the fascination of the long lines of crested breakers like Neptune's racers charging and reforming for the never-ending fray; and, when the unresting tide receded, they have seen the battered hulks of some of the most beautiful ships that ever shaped a course for Wilmington in the days of the Southern Confederacy."

In 1938, however, the Mira-Mar Fishing Pier would be constructed, extending out to cover the sunken *Fanny and Jenny*. That was not by accident. Wrecks often have served as artificial reefs, attracting sea life and thus becoming prime fishing spots. Fishing piers have been built out to wrecks at several locations along the Carolina coast.

The Wrightsville blockade runners were sanded over but still made an appearance from time to time. As recently as 1985, Roderick M. Farb, writing in *Shipwrecks: Diving the*

Graveyard of the Atlantic, noted, "The *Fanny and Jenny* lies about 100 yards north of Masonboro Inlet jetty and about 100 yards offshore in less than 12 feet of water. The visibility underwater is less than three to five feet. Most of the wreck is sanded over, but parts of the hull, the engine, and the boiler are still visible. Winter storms frequently uncover portions of the wreck. Several years ago, scuba divers recovered the *Fanny and Jenny*'s anchor."

At least one item aboard the *Fanny and Jenny*, legend has it, has never been recovered.

The mystery may be unsolvable.

Sprunt wrote, "Captain Coxetter had in his keeping a very valuable gold jewelled sword, which was to be delivered to Gen. R. E. Lee as an expression of the admiration of many prominent English sympathizers. It is still on board this wreck, which lies near a line of breakers to the south of Lumina."

Likewise, half a century later, historian Lewis Philip Hall noted, "A legend says [the *Fanny and Jenny*] carried a handsome cavalry saber with a hilt of solid gold and a beautifully engraved blade. This weapon was a gift from the people of England to a gentleman whom they held in high esteem, General Robert E. Lee, commander of the gallant armies of the Confederate States of America. Many divers in recent years have attempted to recover this magnificent gift, but to date the white shifting sands still guard the treasure."

At about the same time, Rupert L. Benson wrote that the *Fanny and Jenny* "was supposed to have had a gold jeweled headed sword aboard for Jefferson Davis but no one really knew if it was aboard or what happened to it."

John Harden's account added another element to the

story of the mysterious cargo, saying it was responsible for the two deaths. He wrote,

> All hands reached shore safely. But the captain, remembering something that had been trusted to his care and safe-keeping for ultimate delivery, started back to the wreck. His purser went with him. The boat in which they made this impulsive return trip was capsized by belligerent waves and both men drowned.
>
> The story has it that only the captain and the purser knew about the object they went back for. But it was later revealed that aboard the *Fanny and Jennie* was a solid gold, jewel-studded sword bearing this inscription: "To General Robert E. Lee, From his British Sympathisers." There is no record of the sword's ever having been recovered.

Was there such a gold, jeweled sword? Was it intended for Robert E. Lee or Jefferson Davis? How is its existence known?

And of course, was it ever discovered?

The United States Navy's official chronology of the event, compiled by the Navy History Division in 1966, said in part, "*Fanny and Jenny* carried an assorted cargo including a quantity of coal; *Emily* carried a cargo of salt. On *Fanny and Jenny* was also found a solid gold jewel-studded sword inscribed: 'To General Robert E. Lee, from his British sympathizers.'"

But there is no further explanation. How did the navy know of such a sword? How did it know the sword was found?

At least part of the answer lies in two sentences in a second report filed by Commander Crosby on February 11,

1864, two days after the sinking of the *Emily* and the *Fanny and Jenny*. By now, the captured Confederate sailors had been questioned. "The second engineer tells me," Crosby wrote in his official report, "that there was a handsome sword, gold mounted, for General R. E. Lee on board. It was destroyed with the vessel; it was a presentation sword."

And so ends the story, if not the mystery.

It seems unlikely that either the captured Confederates or the Union commander would have made up the existence of a sword. It also seems unlikely the Federal blockaders would have recovered and kept the sword, given that Crosby bothered to report its existence but not its recovery. If the story is true, then, and if no one at the scene recovered it, then the sword went down with the *Fanny and Jenny*.

Either way, the secret is now known only to history—and to the seas.

Chapter Four

"ANOTHER ATLANTIC CITY"

During the summer, Wrightsville Beach is the quintessential resort town. Thousands and thousands of sunbathers and shell seekers share the sands. Families and fishermen share the waters. Drivers share—well, compete for—the parking spaces.

Wrightsville today may seem merely a suburban extension of Wilmington. Expensive homes and upscale shopping pave the way to the beach now, ever encroaching upon what was once an idyllic, serene island. Developers and preservationists disagree on the need to save the past. Developers and environmentalists disagree on saving the island. Old cottages are knocked down, cleared out, and replaced by large new ones. Coming across the drawbridge from the mainland, drivers at first may scarcely be aware this is an island. Suburbia seems to blend seamlessly across the waterway.

But then they reach the beach.

The island is part of North Carolina's chain of beautiful barrier islands, romantic pieces of land that protect the state's coastline and thus turn inhospitable when storms arrive. Wrightsville Beach technically includes the barrier island, which itself is a combination of two islands or four, for those having a longer historical view—as well as the inner Harbor Island and even patches of the mainland. The town, which began as a summer spot for those from nearby Wilmington, was incorporated in 1899.

The name Wrightsville—which attached to Wrightsville Beach long after attaching to a sound, a sound-side village, and an inlet—most likely came from Joshua Grainger Wright (1758–1811), a state legislator and state supreme court justice who owned land along the sound and the coast. It does not, as some suppose, have anything to do with Orville and Wilbur Wright, whose heavier-than-air machine made its first flights on the Outer Banks, to the north.

One Wilmington boy who grew up spending summers on Wrightsville Beach was David Brinkley, the famed televi-

Parking meters and parking stations are nearly as ubiquitous on modern-day Wrightsville Beach as seagulls. This station is at the southern end of the island, near the U.S. Coast Guard facility.

PHOTOGRAPH BY VICKI McALLISTER

sion newscaster. He noted in his autobiography, "In the thirties and forties . . . the East Coast beaches, with the arrival of the automobile, were coming to be crowded, polluted and their waters overfished. Wrightsville escaped most of this because from its beginnings in the nineteenth century it was isolated, off in a corner of the North Carolina coast, no big city nearby and not easily accessible."

Indeed, the push out to Wrightsville from Wilmington was almost incremental—a baby step toward Wrightsville Sound, another onto what is now Harbor Island (then the Hammocks), and finally a third onto the barrier island itself. Even when the island was opened to the public, access was only by train, then later by electric streetcar—the famed beach trolley—or by a footbridge. No automobiles were allowed until 1935.

Automobiles have since made up for lost time. Parking spots are a tough find today in the summer, even though almost all are regulated by parking meters. Not even Brinkley would recognize this Wrightsville. Vacationers fill the three large hotels, the smaller ones, and the modern homes and duplexes for rent. On a sunny holiday weekend, more than 85,000 vehicles cross the bridge. Many seem to drive an endless loop in search of an empty spot. Best advice on a summer weekend: Get here early.

Many do and never return to their cars. Wrightsville may lead the East Coast in walkers per capita. Throughout the town, and on the beach, and especially on The Loop—an exquisite creation—walkers, runners, bicycle riders, and stroller pushers share the paradise that is Wrightsville Beach. Though crowded, Wrightsville remains more congenial than one might expect.

It also remains less commercial than other coastal hot spots, like Nags Head on the Outer Banks and Myrtle Beach across the South Carolina border. In part, this reflects a historical stance against cheesiness. In larger part, it reflects the ever-increasing price of real estate on this thin four-mile strand. Hotels and small shops speckle the island. But it is beach homes—cottages, they are always called—that dominate it. The difference is that today's beach homes are more likely to be duplexes built to the legal limit than the small, quaint cottages of days gone by. Those are an endangered species.

Long before developers and tourists eyed Wrightsville Beach, it was a land of minimal value, the purview of occasional Indians, hunters, fishermen, day adventurers, and campers. And nature, of course. The unspoiled sand and marshes were habitat for all types of creatures—except human beings. The spot was simply too remote, too wild, too without value for man.

Wrightsville Beach showed up as New Hanover Banks on a 1740 map by Robert Hamilton, wrote Lewis Philip Hall in *Land of the Golden River*. It was two distinct bodies of land split by Deep Inlet, which cut through roughly where the Carolina Yacht Club now stands. The Atlantic Ocean was to the east, an unnamed channel to the west. Beyond the channel was what is now Harbor Island, then an unnamed island of 10 acres intersected by two small streams.

Indeed, this ever-shifting barrier island was four separate islands as recently as the early 1800s, before three inlets filled in, two naturally and one with the aid of man. Wrightsville Beach's exterior island now runs from Mason Inlet on the north to Masonboro Inlet on the south and includes what was a separate Shell Island until 1965.

Early visitors were fishermen, campers, and those interested in exploring, wrote the late Rupert L. Benson in his

An electric streetcar line — more often called the beach trolley line — ran up and down the island from 1902 to 1940. The trolley line, which used the tracks of an earlier railroad, lay roughly where South Lumina Avenue is today.
NEW HANOVER PUBLIC LIBRARY, LOUIS T. MOORE COLLECTION

1972 historical narrative of the island. Access was only by boat, through marshland, and over creeks and Banks Channel. Up until about 1900, boats used Wrightsville Inlet, or Moore's Inlet, to get from the Atlantic to the calm waters of Banks Channel. The inlet's closing in 1965 left Masonboro Inlet as the only entry.

The early island was usually referred to as "the Banks," or sometimes as "New Hanover Banks" or "Wrightsville Banks." The only structures on it before the middle of the 19th century were seasonal fishing shacks, the word *structures* perhaps overstating the reality. In time, a real building arrived, the Carolina Yacht Club in 1853. Hauling materials to the island must have been difficult, but labor was available. As *The State* magazine noted a century later, "Nine years before the beginning of the devastating War Between the States, and more than a decade prior to Lincoln's Emancipation Proclamation, Negro slaves furnished the manpower for the erection of Wrightsville's first building." A map of the period shows only the clubhouse on the island, labeled both "Banks House" and "CYC." Though it has moved, the Carolina Yacht Club remains on the island and is one of the oldest continuously operating yacht clubs in America, having begun just nine years after the oldest, the New York Yacht Club.

The historic Carolina Yacht Club grew from races and arguments over whose yacht was the best, Norwood Giles, Esq., wrote in 1887. The new club expanded quickly. Giles noted that, by 1860,

> We not only had regattas, but bank parties. The whole society of Masonboro and Wrightsville Beach would meet on the beach and enjoy an entire day, returning by moonlight. This last was arranged by the young ladies. Ah! Many an old barnacle studded turtle was puzzled to know what animal made such curious tracks as were left by some happy couples strolling up the beach. . . . No wonder that the present generation of sand crabs have prominent eyes, when we consider the astonishment experienced by their ancestors at such a carrying on. Not only were these bank parties social gatherings, but a time to display huge watermelons and delicious fruit. A pleasant sight it was, I warrant you, to see the small boys with brilliant noses and indescribable straw hats, down to their ears in luscious rinds.

The club ceased operation from 1861 to 1865, for obvious reasons. "At the age of our prosperity," Giles wrote, "the tide of war swept over the land and carried off many of our best members and boats. The military took possession of our yachts and at roll call after the war [16 yachts] failed to respond." The first regatta after the Civil War was held July 4, 1865. But for the next six years, during Reconstruction, "the times were such as to forbid much sport or recreation." By 1887, the club, still the island's only occupant, had grown to 130 members.

During those years, fishermen, boaters, and yacht-club members remained the island's primary visitors. Access still was only by water. It would be decades after the clubhouse's construction before other transportation, or anything that might be called growth, reached Wrightsville.

The first step was a road out from the city. The Wilmington & Coast Turnpike, authorized by a general-assembly charter in 1875, was an eight-mile road that suddenly made the coast more accessible.

The new road out from Wilmington quickly received an upgrade. By 1887, it was topped with oyster shells and operated as a toll road. The striking white turnpike, graded and ditched on both sides, became known as the Shell Road. The road could be problematic for horse-drawn carriages; periodically, journeys had to be stopped so pieces of shell could be removed from horses' hooves. But the glittering shell turnpike was an attraction in itself. "At that time it was the prettiest shell road in America," Benson wrote, "and one of the things all Wilmingtonians pointed to with a just feeling of pride."

The road opened up what had become the resort village of Wrightsville, located on the sound within sight of the beach. As early as 1880, one visitor, a Mr. Henkel of New Market, Virginia, wrote, "This village is destined to become another Atlantic City. Already many hundreds of people come here and spend the hot summer months. They rough it, finding good, plain, table fare at twenty-five dollars per month. Many sleep in hammocks out of doors, and dress is very plain. The bathing for men, women and children is almost constant, and most are excellent swimmers. Men are to be seen with broad brimmed hats, in rough, loose fitting, flannel suits, which are used for dress and bathing suits."

"The Playground of the South" was what promoters called it.

Bigger things were to come. In 1888, the Wilmington

and Seacoast Railroad was built from downtown Wilmington to Wrightsville Sound and on over the marshlands of the sound to the Hammocks. The railroad went up rapidly. Ground was broken on February 13, 1888, and construction was completed by June 15. That included the erection of the high, mile-long trestle across the tidal marsh of Wrightsville Sound to the Hammocks. All that was left was the final touch, a solid silver spike driven by railroad president William Latimer at the dedication ceremony. A Wilmington newspaper later recounted the day:

> At 4:30 in the afternoon of June 17, 1888, a large crowd of nicely dressed ladies, gentlemen and children gathered at the Front Street depot of the Wilmington & Weldon Railroad. There on a siding, stood one of the handsome, new, gilt embellished and brass-trimmed steam engines and its string of fine appointed and upholstered, canary-colored passenger coaches of the Wilmington & Sea Coast Railroad. Soon after the train and its eager passengers were flying toward the Sound and Hammocks, via the connection of Brunswick Street. Arriving at the terminus of the railroad on the Hammocks, where a large crowd had assembled, by way of sharpies and other sailing craft, Mr. W. I. Chadbourn, the contractor, formally turned over the railroad to its manager. At the conclusion of his speech Mr. Chadbourn said, "As I have said, the road is completed, yet one thing is lacking—a single spike—and all is done. May this spike, in its purity and value, be symbolic of the future of this little road."

Symbolically and practically, it was a big road. The final step to the coast was now only a matter of time.

It came quickly. Already in 1888, the Island Beach Hotel was under way on the Hammocks, the triangular-shaped inner island. But the big push was to the banks alongside the Atlantic Ocean. A footbridge was built across Banks Channel, meaning vacationers now could ride the train from Wilmington out to the Hammocks, then walk across to the beach. Two men from the town of Chadbourn, J. A. Brown and R. E. L. Brown, took advantage. They built a restaurant and men's and women's bathhouses on the beach in the summer of 1888. They were the island's first buildings since the yacht club 32 years earlier.

But there was nothing else. In a newspaper interview nearly four decades later, then-mayor J. A. Taylor remembered that the only source of fresh water was a spring that was covered when the tide rose. At low tide, those camping on the beach would bring all the small vessels they had to fill with enough fresh water to use until the tide again subsided. Others, afraid of drinking from the small hole, brought their water from Wilmington.

"To go to the beach was to go rustic," Taylor said. "No one has a bath suit—there weren't any such things. The women went in bathing in skirts and stockings when the men went to town to work."

The train soon came to the beach as well. The construction of another trestle, this across Banks Channel to the beach, began the day after New Year's in 1889. It was the work of a new company, the Sea View Railroad Company, which would reorganize shortly into the Ocean View Railroad Company. After the mile-and-a-half connection was complete, the company built tracks south to Masonboro Inlet along the path of what is now South Lumina Avenue.

On May 21, 1889, the aptly named Ocean View Railroad began operation. Passengers leaving Wilmington on the Seacoast Railroad now could change to the Ocean View at the Hammocks for the trip to the beach. The Ocean

View's passenger cars for summer were open-sided, though each had a waterproof curtain for unexpected showers. The steam train, taken to the end, stopped within 50 yards of the ocean.

An unnamed passenger described his wondrous first trip: "There is, of course, a magnificent view out to sea all along the line, and passengers can sit in their seats, as the train glides up the beach, and look far out over the swelling blue expanse of waters until they kiss the distant horizon. On the other hand stretches the series of sounds and marshes of the environments, and as far as the eye can reach there will be in summer an alternating green and shimmering winding of waters that make up a view very rare indeed. Across the serpentine sounds and stretches of marshes, Wrightsville may also be seen, with her pretty cottages straggling up the Sound, half-hidden in the live oaks."

The railroad, later sold to the Wilmington and Seacoast Railroad, was not merely the tool by which the island was opened. It became an iconic image. Benson, writing in the early 1970s, quoted an older resident as saying, "This train was a sight to behold with its wood burning engine and long string of side entrance passenger cars and flat freight cedars puffing along majestically. I am told that the first engine of this famous Railroad blew up one day, but fortunately with no loss of life, and a new engine was purchased to continue the daily runs for the delight and pleasure of the citizens and visitors coming from far and wide." The new locomotive was named Bessie, apparently for the niece of railroad president William Latimer. Bessie became a household word.

Not surprisingly, the newly opened resort island was called Ocean View Beach. Construction proceeded at break-neck pace. Three train stations went up: Station One, where the tracks turned sharply south after coming over from the Hammocks, plus stations at the yacht club and at the end of the line. This latter was known as the Masonboro terminus or Switchback Station. Here was built the island's first hotel, the Breeze House, which, in his newspaper interview nearly four decades later, then-mayor Taylor said was known as the Mayo House. The hotel, opened on July 2, 1889, included an 80-by-30-foot dining area advertised as "Ocean View Dining Rooms at Switchback Station."

Everything moved quickly.

The island's first big holiday was just two days later, on July 4, 1889. Some 2,085 persons visited that day, taking 50-cent round-trip train rides between Wilmington and Ocean View. The yacht club held a regatta in Wrightsville Sound. The visitors enjoyed a tub race across Banks Channel, a shooting gallery, and merry-go-rounds at both Ocean View and the Hammocks. Couples danced to string bands in pavilions at Ocean View and the Hammocks. A ball was held that night on the Hammocks in the ballroom of the Island Beach Hotel. Fireworks began at 8 P.M., the largest display exploding near midnight.

Railroads had made the island accessible. Paradise was now available to the common man—at least the common man of moderate means. Now, those desiring the ocean life—or those desiring to sell to those who desired the ocean life—began swarming the narrow piece of land. Handsome beachfront cottages were built. So was a second small hotel on the beach, the Atlas House. Bathhouses and pavilions were constructed.

Life on the island was both exciting and idyllic. There were, however, occasional intrusions into this bliss.

The first drowning occurred less than six weeks after the Ocean View Railroad began running. Claude M. Lockhart, described in a newspaper article as "the handsome young assistant clerk at Orton House in the city," went into the ocean at Brown Bath House with two friends on Sunday afternoon,

South Lumina Avenue today, sans tracks. The island has since been widened and, to the right in the photograph, lies Waynick Boulevard.
PHOTOGRAPH BY VICKI McALLISTER

July 1, 1889. He became exhausted in the rough surf. One friend struggled with Lockhart while the other went for help. Three men arrived and tried to get a lifeline through the surf, but the friend could hold his grip no longer. Lockhart sank from view. A few days later, owner J. A. Brown announced he was putting in lifelines to circle the 500 feet of beach in front of his bathhouses. He would also keep several lifeboats, one of them manned. In 1913, the town would require large hotels and clubs to provide lifeguards and surf boats as well.

Even more disturbing was the disappearance six years after Lockhart's death of an eight-year-old boy, Harry Teboe. Lewis Philip Hall, citing a cousin of Teboe's father, Mrs. I. S. King of Wilmington, told the story, which he called "The Mystery of Ocean View Beach."

In July 1895, young Harry went to the beach with his married older sister, Emma Turney. They rode the train from Wilmington to Ocean View Beach, the two of them and Harry's little dog, and checked in at the Atlas House. The next morning, July 25, Harry and his dog went out with his new pail and shovel to play. At lunch, Emma went looking for Harry but couldn't find him.

The fear was that he had drowned. One person reported hearing cries for help from the roaring surf. But others had seen a boy fitting Harry's description with a man and woman at a train depot in Wilmington. It seemed likely that he had been kidnapped. Harry's dog met every train that arrived on the beach after his disappearance. Phillip and Dora Teboe were desperate to find their son. Telegraph descriptions were dispatched. The state's newspapers joined in a massive search. Nothing came of it.

One day 25 years later, Robert Hayes, home in Hauto, Pennsylvania, was reading the "Missing Persons" column of a detective magazine. Details of one item, about Harry Teboe, sounded familiar. He contacted Dora Teboe, now living in Charleston, South Carolina. Over a series of letters, they realized he was indeed the missing son. After being kidnapped, Harry had been overtaken by fever and lost some of his memory. The kidnappers, he said, treated him cruelly. When he was 12, he was forced to work in a factory. Two years later, he ran away to join the navy. When America entered World War I, his ship was put on active duty. Wounded in battle at sea, he was hospitalized in France. There, he met his future wife; the couple was married in Allentown, Pennsylvania. Now, finally, Harry was reunited with his family. At a reunion in Charleston, Mr. and Mrs. Robert Hayes were married again, this time as Mr. and Mrs. Harry Teboe.

Wrightsville Beach continued its explosive growth as the end of the 19th century neared. A large hotel was needed quickly. The Seashore Hotel was planned as a two-story structure, but plans were bumped up. The three-story Seashore was built in two months. It opened on June 15, 1897, alongside Station Three and the railroad tracks, at the same spot where the Blockade Runner would go more than six decades later.

The Colonial-style cream-and-white Seashore had 150 rooms and fireplaces, plus a 40-by-108-foot dining room, all surrounded by a veranda that was 15 feet wide and 800 feet long. It was still too small. The following winter, a 30-room annex was built, along with a 350-by-150-foot pavilion with wide porches and balconies, as well as men's and women's bathhouses. In 1900, the Seashore would expand again.

The Seashore became the island's early showplace. Benson, apparently quoting from the *Wilmington Messenger* of August 22, 1897, noted,

> It was erected right on the Ocean front where the Ocean spray from the breakers almost dashed upon the plazas. It was handsomely furnished for that day with Waterworks and modern improvements for its guests. It is also noted that the attractions of Wrightsville Beach surpassed those of any resort in America, with its unsurpassed surf for Ocean bathing and Banks Channel for still water bathing and boating and yachting facilities deluxe. The facilities afforded for fishing were the finest, with Pig fish, seabass, Sheephead, Black fish, Blue fish, Spanish Mackerel and many others abounding in the waters luring the fishermen. . . . The Sound waters also abounded in deliciously flavored oysters, clams, crabs and other species. The marsh lands to the west between Banks Channel and the mainland afford a sportsman's paradise for the hunters. Marsh hen being plentiful, and also deer driving

on the mainland for additional sport. The Resort with its Hotels, bath houses, handsome cottages, Railroad facilities, (with up to twenty-five trains a day, as the occasion required), Water and sewer, telephone service, two free mail deliveries a day, vehicular traffic over the Turnpike to Wrightsville Sound all at the very door steps of Wilmington, which is very fortunate above all other cities in America, and destined to become famous throughout the country.

Building continued. The Atlas Hotel burned in March 1897 and was replaced in June 1899 by the two-story, 30-room Ocean View Hotel. The Ocean View had broad porches and a dining room facing the ocean.

The Ocean View Railroad began operation in 1889, taking visitors to the ocean side for the first time. Ocean View Beach, as Wrightsville was then called, became a summer resort with a new pavilion, with small hotels and restaurants. This photograph was taken about the turn of the 20th century.

NEW HANOVER PUBLIC LIBRARY, LOUIS T. MOORE COLLECTION

Another yacht club appeared on the island, the Clarendon, its clubhouse located between the Seashore Hotel and the end of the tracks. The Clarendon was incorporated in 1895 with five members. It changed its name to the Atlantic Yacht Club and by 1897 had 170 members.

This narrow, deserted island had become a summer community. An 1897 listing showed 41 cottages—including that of Colonel F. W. Forster, the first on the island—three hotels, two yacht clubs, the Shelter of the Silver Cross, and various bathhouses. Telephone service was extended to the island.

By 1899, the need for organization became apparent. The town of Wrightsville Beach was incorporated on March 6, 1899. A winter watchman was hired.

The resort town was booming now, well on its way to becoming another Atlantic City or better. Almost nothing, it seemed, could stop "the Playground of the South" as the new century neared.

Almost nothing.

The Seashore Hotel, which opened in 1897, was the island's first major hotel and quickly became a popular spot. Hotel-goers swam in the Atlantic Ocean, day or night, as this early 1900s post card shows. The Blockade Runner Resort Hotel is now the third major hotel at the location.

AUTHOR COLLECTION

Chapter Five

THE STORM OF 1899

The wind picked up late in the evening on Monday, October 30, 1899. The tide was advancing. The rains came.

The new town of Wrightsville Beach was in for a pounding.

Hurricanes weren't yet called hurricanes. But it soon became clear what sort of power this storm was carrying. The island had been hit by a frightening electrical storm four months earlier, on June 29. The roof of the Seashore Hotel was struck twice by lightning bolts, and the roof of M. J. Corbett's cottage was struck by a bolt that ran down the wall, shattered a window, and stunned three women in an upper room. Two of the women were injured by flying fragments of wood, and the other fell unconscious. The island's phone exchanges were briefly knocked out, and a Southern Bell exchange operator even received a severe shock while making a connection.

But this was something different.

The storm of 1899—or "the Big Storm," as it became colloquially known—was a full-fledged hurricane. It was born of an unfortunate combination of factors, much like Hurricane Hazel 55 years later. High-powered winds made the storm treacherous in itself. Worse, it would hit the island at high tide. Now, in addition to the winds and rains, flooding would be a problem. The island would be both battered and overrun.

The storm would not reach its full intensity until the early-morning hours, shortly before sunrise. Even now during the evening, though, the wind roared. The rain pounded. The surf flew. Trees were blown sideways, then uprooted. Cottages were bludgeoned into submission.

Fortunately, the island was nearly empty. Beach season had passed, and few people were still in the hotels and cottages. For the most part, only fishermen visited in October, and most were gone by nightfall. The caretakers and laborers who tended the cottages during the off-season were still about, however. They now faced rapidly rising waters. Jay Barnes, in *North Carolina's Hurricane History*, wrote that many faced close calls. The janitor at the Carolina Club House wisely abandoned the beach at midnight, before the storm reached full intensity. It was bad enough. He jumped into a small skiff and sailed to his home in Hewlett's Creek, later describing his ordeal as "terrific in the extreme."

For others, it was worse. Henry Brewington, a watchman for the Ocean View Hotel and several cottages, was forced onto the roof of the Russell Cottage by the rising storm. The cottage collapsed. Brewington swam through the rushing waters to the Atlantic Yacht Club, where his nightmare continued. It, too, was about to collapse. Brewington took off again, this time to swim to safety by reaching the trestle at Wrightsville Station.

No place was safe for long, though. By the time J. T. Dooley, the railroad section master who lived on the Hammocks, got to the trestle, even it was endangered. Dooley hurriedly gathered up his wife and three children.

They crossed the railway bridge at 3:30 A.M.

The bridge collapsed at 4 A.M.

The island fared as badly. Barrier islands are nature's storm absorbers, and Wrightsville was absorbing a big one. In many locations, the island ceased to exist during the hours of the storm. Ocean waves simply washed over it, blending the Atlantic Ocean and Banks Channel into one large, churning pool. Worse, the waves sometimes carried cottages with them, sweeping them into the channel.

It was not until much later in the day on October 31, Halloween, that the people of Wilmington were able to assess the damage. A large and apprehensive crowd boarded the Seacoast train at 2:30 that afternoon for the ride to the coast. They thought they were prepared for the worst. Most were not. The train rounded the curve before Wrightsville Station. The final turn brought into view the long trestle leading from the mainland to the Hammocks and on to Wrightsville Beach. Those on board were horrified. They had not counted on this. The train screeched to a stop. A reporter from the *Wilmington Messenger* wrote,

> The massive railroad trestle was warped and twisted, and for a few hundred (feet) extending from the station towards the Hammocks the rails and ties were torn from the piles, and presented a tangled wreck piled down in the waters of the sound. The railroad tracks, approaching the station as far toward the city as the Pritchard cottage, was warped and torn and the large platform surrounding the depot was piled high with seaweed and other drift. To the right and left, stretching around the shore of the sound, as far as the eye could reach, where but yesterday, as it were, the famous shell road wound in beautiful curves, was a mass of

deep tangled debris of every conceivable kind, the wreckage of cottages from the beach and of boats and bath houses along the shore of the sound.

Destruction on the island was enormous. The southern portion had been overrun. More than 20 cottages were either washed into the sound or demolished. So, too, was the Shelter of the Silver Cross, a summer home for invalid women and children built by the Ministering Circle of the King's Daughters. Shops, hotels, clubs, and docks were destroyed. Notable among them were the Ocean View Hotel, the old Hewlett barroom south of the hotel, and the new public pavilion north of the Seashore Hotel. The Carolina Yacht Club and the Atlantic Yacht Club both were washed from their foundations and carried by the tides.

Much of the railroad track was unusable. The track south of Station Three had been swept into Banks Channel. The crossties stuck up from the water like picket fencing.

Figures help tell the devastation of the Big Storm. Total property values on Wrightsville Beach had reached $71,366 in 1899, its first year as an incorporated town. Contractor and builder Thad Tyler estimated the beach had suffered $50,000 worth of damage, and the railroad another $25,000.

Worse, perhaps, was the damage to Wrightsville's push to become a major resort—to its hopes and dreams, even to its psyche. The storm was disturbing. Even discounting the June electrical storm, this was the second severe hurricane of the 1899 season—one in August had caused extensive damage elsewhere in the state—marking the fourth time in less than 20 years that two monsters had visited North Carolina in one year. "Some even speculated," Barnes noted, "that these violent storms were God's punishment to the citizens for allowing dancing on Sundays in local clubs."

On Wrightsville Beach, people had to be wondering, Can we rebuild? Is it worth trying?

Rebuilding began almost immediately.

The Carolina Yacht Club, which had to be rebuilt entirely, was among the first to emerge from the ruins. A large two-story clubhouse reopened on June 13, 1900. This one, U-shaped, faced Banks Channel, its covered walk reaching west to the boardwalk. The new clubhouse had a ballroom, a men's lounge and bar, dressing rooms for everyone, and large porches. Likewise, the Atlantic Yacht Club had to be entirely rebuilt, and likewise, it included improvements; a two-story clubhouse larger than its predecessor opened on June 29, 1900.

Wrightsville marched onward. Old buildings were replaced. New ones went up. A 400-seat vaudeville theater, the Casino, was built for $2,500. It opened for the 1902 season, putting on afternoon and evening performances throughout the summer. For the Fourth of July, it offered performances at noon, 4 P.M., and 8 P.M. and had music and dancing as well. The Fourth, of course, was a busy day. Twenty trains ran to the island that day. The Atlantic and Carolina yacht clubs engaged in a regatta, the Wilmington Division of the North Carolina Naval Brigade conducted a drill, and the Seashore Hotel had morning and afternoon concerts, followed by a grand ball in the evening. Fireworks were shot off at 9:30 P.M. at the Hammocks.

The Casino was built for "polite vaudeville" and light opera. But by the 1904 season, it began offering a new favorite, short "moving pictures," usually six to eight an evening. A June 29 article in the *Wilmington Star* highlighted a couple,

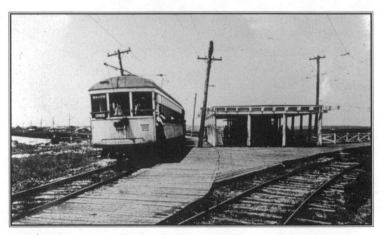

After the Storm of 1899, Wrightsville Beach set about rebuilding. The 1902 conversion of a rail line to an electric streetcar line proved hugely popular. The new beach trolleys brought visitors and development. Here a beach car heads south from Station One, the first stop after crossing onto the outer island.

NEW HANOVER PUBLIC LIBRARY, ROBERT M. FALES COLLECTION

including *Phantom Railway*, which put the viewer up front of a train traveling at 60 miles an hour, no small feat more than a century ago. It was, the paper breathlessly assured its readers,

> a very excellent moving picture taken from the cow-catcher of a locomotive on the railroad from Monte Carlo. This line passes through a mountainous country which is full of curves and tunnels. As the picture springs into view on the screen, the track with cross-ties and over-hanging cliffs rushes towards you at a terrific speed, passing from time to time around sharp curves and under the base of huge rocks. Suddenly a tunnel appears in the distance and, as the train rushes toward the opening, it becomes larger and larger. There is a dash into darkness and then in the extreme end of the tun-

nel a faint glimmer of light appears which eventually widens into an opening as the train again reappears into daylight. From time to time during the trip the onlooker is given a glimpse of the interior of the coaches and a newly wedded couple are seen in one of the compartments.

But the big news at Wrightsville Beach was trolleys.

The Wilmington and Seacoast Railroad was merged into Wilmington's gaslight company and its street railway company in 1902. Hugh MacRae, whose banking and brokerage house negotiated the deal, was president of the new Consolidated Railways, Light and Power Company. What the new company would do, he had confirmed to an inquiring reporter the previous summer, was convert the trains to electric streetcars, or trolleys. That would extend the streetcar lines from downtown Wilmington, allowing passengers to ride straight through on the trolleys and actually decreasing their cost.

Trolleys!

Few changes to the island would make more of an impact than trading the puffing steam-engine railroad cars for electric trolleys. The Hanover Seaside Club, for instance, would build a second clubhouse on Wrightsville. Organized as a German social club, it had begun in 1898 at Carolina Beach. But now with the electric cars, getting to Wrightsville from Wilmington was simply more convenient than getting to Carolina Beach.

Converting to streetcars took the laying of miles of new track in Wilmington and improvements to the rail line to the beach. Work was done quickly to catch as much of the 1902 summer season as possible. Consolidated, which had built the Casino theater, went full-throttle on all fronts. It ordered four new 53-passenger, state-of-the-art beach cars, twice as big as regular streetcars. Overhead cable was strung. The first trolley rode the rails of the Seacoast Railroad to the Carolina Yacht Club on July 25, 1902. Within a few days, the rest of the line was wired. Trolleys could go all the way south to the Masonboro terminus.

Trains were now a thing of the past on Wrightsville Beach. Trolley cars were here. Some called them "electric streetcars," as the smaller city cars in Wilmington were known. More called them "beach trolley cars" or simply "beach cars." A family could get on the line in Wilmington and ride the eight miles in about 45 minutes or less. The impact was evident throughout the island. More homes were built, most in a single row along the ocean. Other improvements followed quickly. Electric lights soon appeared.

A new hotel, one to rival and even surpass the Seashore, made its appearance. The luxurious Tarrymoore opened on

Hotel Tarrymore, Wrightsville Beach, Wilmington, N. C.

Wrightsville's first large upscale hotel was the Tarrymoore, opened by W.J. Moore in 1905. There were 125 rooms, many of them luxury suites and most with a view of the ocean. Lettering on the hotel itself read "Hotel Tarrymoore." But the title of this postcard calls it the "Tarrymore."
AUTHOR COLLECTION

Half a dozen years after opening, the Tarrymoore was sold and renamed the Oceanic. Among the improvements was the adding of a distinctive tower. The hotel was the social center of what was then the northern end of the island, with fine dining, dancing, and concerts.
AUTHOR COLLECTION

June 6, 1905, on what was then the north end of the island, near Station One. The Tarrymoore's developer, W. J. Moore of Charlotte, seems to have had a sense of humor in incorporating his name into the hotel's and perhaps turning upside down the biblical exhortation to "tarry no more." Indeed, a popular 19th-century hymn began, "O love that casts out fear/O love that casts out sin/Tarry no more without/But come and dwell within."

Vacationers soon flocked to dwell within the new Tarrymoore. It had 125 elegantly furnished rooms, nearly all of which faced the sea. Many were suites with private baths, telephones, and electric lights. The Tarrymoore had its own 200-foot well to draw water from an artesian spring. Daily concerts and dancing were held in the 4,000-square-foot dining room.

Moore eventually sold the hotel to a group of Wilmington businessmen in 1911–12. Two wings were added, and the striking V-shaped structure was renamed the Oceanic Hotel. A distinctive tower was erected. The hotel began running sailboat excursions for its guests. The Oceanic was the social center of the northern half of the island.

But nothing—not the new Tarrymoore, not electric lights, not moving pictures, not even the new beach trolleys— lit up the island the way one famous newcomer would.

Chapter Six

LUMINA

"The Fun Spot of the South," this summer entertainment pavilion was to be, and the Consolidated Railways, Light and Power Company spared no expense to make it that.

It overshot the mark.

Lumina became much more.

Three or four generations of beachgoers, of fun seekers, of families, of students, of working people, of executives, of young lovers, of older lovers, of North Carolinians, of Southerners, of Easterners would make many of their greatest memories at this spot. They would arrive by train, later by trolley, and later still by car. They came during two world wars. They came before, between, and after the wars. They played in the surf, watched athletic contests in the surf, watched movies in the surf. They danced the one-step, the two-step, the waltz, then later the tango and the turkey trot, then later the Rag and the Castle Walk. They danced the shag. They danced the foxtrot and even the square dance. They danced the jitterbug. They listened to Robert J. Weidemeyer and his orchestra, Jelly Leftwich and his orchestra, and the famous Big Bands: Jimmy Dorsey, Tommy Dorsey, Sammy Kay, Guy

Lombardo, Stan Kenton, Kay Kyser.

Just the name would light up the island, would light up summers, would light up lives and, later, memories.

Lumina.

Hugh MacRae and other officers of Consolidated decided on *Lumina* because it brought to mind *luminescent*, the Latin word for *lights*, the plural of *lumen*.

Several thousand incandescent bulbs lighted the pavilion at night, just in case the message wasn't clear.

The June 7, 1905, *Wilmington Dispatch* explained:

"LUMINA" THE NAME
Handsome New Pavilion Has Been Given an
Appropriate Title

Suggestive of the great brilliancy at night, or suggested by that brilliance the new pavilion at Wrightsville Beach has been named the "Lumina." By that title it will be known and it is a very appropriate and very attractive one. The building when completed will contain 1,000 incandescent lights, arc lights outside and a powerful search light in the tower of the building. There is no doubt about the pavilion being the largest and most up-to-date of its kind in the South. It will prove a great attraction this season.

The Lumina Pavilion was in essence a 12,500-square-foot entertainment center, ocean park, and dance floor. When they opened the doors of Lumina on June 3, 1905, the owners may as well have been opening Disney World, Las Vegas, and the Super Bowl all rolled into one for that early-20th-century audience. People had never seen anything like it.

The Lumina Pavilion opened on June 3, 1905, transforming Wrightsville Beach from a fledgling resort to an entertainment capital. Lumina was a 12,500-square-foot entertainment center, ocean park, and dance floor. A Wilmington paper raved in advance of its arrival: "There is no doubt about the pavilion being the largest and most up-to-date of its kind in the South. It will prove a great attraction this season." The rave would prove a huge understatement.

NEW HANOVER PUBLIC LIBRARY, ROBERT M. FALES COLLECTION

Pavilion was a commonly used term then, usually applied to a large building for athletics or entertainment. But this was no common pavilion. It was built at the whopping cost of $6,000 to $7,000, according to the *Wilmington Dispatch*, which gushed about the "giant hall of amusement." The elaborate two-story structure was built to a football-field length of 300 feet. The ground floor included a bowling alley, a shooting gallery, a broad promenade with refreshments and lunch booths on one side and slot machines and sundry amusements on the other. Both free bathrooms and more elaborate nickel bathrooms were available. A broad stairway led to a 50-by-70-foot second-floor ballroom, also used as a skating rink, encircled by a 15-foot-wide promenade for seating and with an orchestra balcony at the south end. A restaurant with open fireplaces for winter was at the north end. A 15-piece orchestra played concerts and also provided dance music each night during the summer.

Word quickly spread of the new hot spot, which was advertised as "the People's Pleasure Palace." Within weeks of its opening, an out-of-town newspaper already reported, "Gay and brilliant Lumina, whose fame has spread to the cradle of American Independence in Mecklenburg [County, North Carolina], was alive with humanity yesterday afternoon and until late last night. The big excursion from Charlotte, despite the fact that it was a Sunday School excursion, was not averse to 'tripping the light fantastic,' and joined merrily in the pleasure of the evening."

Train excursions with 10 to 15 cars full of Lumina-goers

The dance floor was flag-bedecked and packed on summer evenings. Proper attire was required for dancers to get in the door. Proper decorum was required once on the dance floor to stay there — and chaperons patrolled the floor to make sure.
NEW HANOVER PUBLIC LIBRARY, ROBERT M. FALES COLLECTION

soon were coming almost daily to Wilmington. They arrived from three states and from as far away as Atlanta. Wilmington society and Wrightsville residents flocked there as well. Many Lumina-goers were summer vacationers renting a cottage or staying in one of the hotels or boardinghouses.

They kept coming, for the entertainment and especially the dancing. While an orchestra played on summer evenings, a chaperon and her assistants prowled the floor to make sure decorum was maintained. Admission was free in those early years, though of course Consolidated received trolley fares from everyone coming to the island.

The *Wilmington Messenger* of July 20, 1905, reported that, on the previous night, Lumina had the largest number of dancers of the season, but then that was hardly news: "This pleasure palace grows in popularity nightly and each night brings larger crowds than the preceding night."

What didn't Lumina have? The *Messenger* headlined an article on July 26, "A NOVEL CAMERA. Photoscope at Lumina Presents You With Your Picture in Five Seconds by Dropping a Nickel in Slot and Looking at Machine."

Phonograph record players were introduced in the fall, apparently during orchestra breaks. The *Messenger* of October 28, 1905, trumpeted that Saturday night's dance at Lumina, which stayed open throughout the fall:

> The chilly blasts of winter only make the interior of Lumina more cheerful and with the huge fire place gives it the appearance of some large hotel corridor. There is nothing more delightful than to sit in this large pavilion and look out over the ocean. The cooler the day the more pleasant it is. . . .
>
> The new talking machine will be introduced tonight for the first time. Those who go down tonight will be surprised to hear the clearness and distinct-

ness with which the songs and music are rendered and especially when the machine is in such a large hall as the one at Lumina.

It seemed every detail was attended to. During summer weekends and holidays, a surf boat with six lifeguards was anchored just beyond the breakers of the packed beach. The heavily used hardwood dance floor was waxed and polished twice a week. The entire building was redecorated nearly every month with flags and banners in the American red, white, and blue, as well as the Confederate battle flag. Every two years, Lumina was repainted a soft green with white trim. The promenades were gray.

Lumina's light got brighter year by year. Capacity crowds filled, then overflowed the facility. Expansion was a necessity. MacRae's Consolidated, reorganized into the Tide Water Power Company in 1907, obliged for the 1909 season.

The new "Greater Lumina" was just that. One report claimed the second floor alone now had 25,000 square feet of space, plus another 6,000 for the verandas. To be sure, the ballroom virtually doubled in size, to 50 by 120 feet. A new 20-musician orchestra shell, constructed on the west side, was scientifically enhanced for perfect acoustics. The luminescent ballroom had state-of-the-art lighting—15 brilliant tungsten lights of 200 candlepower each.

"Greater Lumina" drew even greater crowds of visitors, many of whom rented a bathing suit for a dime a day and then had to pay a quarter for a shower. On July 4, 1910, the Tide Water Power Company's streetcars ran all day, bringing a record-breaking 5,000 people to Wrightsville Beach for the holiday. More than 3,000 of them came to Lumina. Many danced that evening to the 16-piece orchestra of John F. Kneissel, a Lumina favorite.

In 1911, the Tide Water Power Company upped the

illumination again, this time placing some 600 incandescent lights around the exterior of the pavilion. The brilliance could be seen for miles, which proved an unexpected aid to ships along North Carolina's treacherous coast. Generations of sailors would use Lumina as a nautical beacon.

The overhead ballroom lights were replaced in 1914, the *Wilmington Star* reported, "with a new type of nitrogen lamps. The new lights are of the very latest type." The 11 lights each carried 550 candlepower, doubling the output of the old lighting.

From the top of its roof to the ground, inside and out, Lumina was figuratively and now almost literally ablaze.

It continued growing. The verandas on the south side were extended in 1910. Some 150 bath and shower rooms were added for beachgoers in 1911, bringing the total to nearly 400. In 1913, a 250-foot-long terrace was wrapped around three sides of the building, in essence becoming a third deck that later would be nicknamed "the Hurricane Deck." It gave Lumina an additional 7,100 square feet of floor space. A 138-foot bridge was extended from the deck across the double rail tracks below, leading down to a boardwalk to Banks Channel. At the same time, Lumina was extended 45 feet toward the ocean, increasing the seating capacity from 590 to 1,420.

The extension toward the ocean also created a unique movie theater. Tide Water Power erected a large movie screen in the surf, extended high into the air on pilings. Silent movies, usually comedies or Westerns, were projected to 300 people in tiered seating on the high, new terrace. They got two shows for the price of one—the movie and, behind it, the majestic, moonlit sea.

When the tide was low, a second theater of sorts opened up for the ocean movies. Beachgoers dropped themselves on the sand beneath the terrace seats, sometimes bringing blankets or even orange-crate seats, and watched the likes of

Fatty Arbuckle and Mabel Norman for free as their children played.

The cream of Wilmington society was frequently on view for Lumina patrons, mingling easily with the middle class. The observant might also have noticed a young man with movie-star looks on the premises from time to time. Randolph Scott befriended a local boy, Andrew H. Harriss, Jr., at a boarding school in Virginia. They sailed together in 1914, when Scott was 16. "Randy Scott became a frequent visitor in the Harriss household at Summer Rest on Wrightsville Sound," wrote Anne Russell in *The Carolina Yacht Club Chronicles*. "The two young men partied at Lumina, swam in the ocean, and enjoyed the amenities of the Carolina Yacht Club." The friendship continued when the two went off to World War I. Scott, of course, would go on to become a motion-picture star for generations.

Friday night was always Children's Night at Lumina, which allowed kids under 12 free admission. They were free to enjoy a comedy on the indoor movie screen, souvenirs, games, and events. There was much to do. An aquarium held 50 varieties of fish. A large water slide ran into Banks Channel.

For athletically inclined adults, the pavilion held three major athletics and aquatics meets every summer. Lumina even managed to bring in outside events. One occasion was the July 4, 1919, world heavyweight boxing "fight of the century," in which Jack Dempsey knocked out Jess Willard. A blow-by-blow description was received by telegraph from ringside at Toledo, Ohio. Each dispatch was given to Lumina's large, muscular dance-floor manager and lifeguard, W. B. "Tuck" Savage. He read them aloud from the veranda to the thousands of people on the beach and in the ocean.

But dancing was the thing. Bands played nightly for the enchanted couples. By 1914, ragtime music and the dance steps that followed were accepted at Lumina. The waltz was soon replaced by the tango, the turkey trot, the maxixe, the Australian crawl, and others. The next year, classes were taught in the new Castle Walk, in which the man quickly walked his partner backwards.

By the 1920s, large bands were making their way to Lumina. Robert J. Weidemeyer and his orchestra, hailing from Huntington, West Virginia, played throughout each summer from 1924 to 1929, performing for nightly dances as well as free concerts each Sunday afternoon and night. Weidemeyer's orchestra also furnished the nightly dinner music at the Oceanic Hotel. At Lumina, the orchestra would play old favorites and new popular music to appeal to dancers of varied ages—songs like "Some Times I'm Happy," "Hallelujah," "Jericho," "It Had to Be You," "Old Man River," "Sweet Georgia Brown," "If You Knew Susie," and "Who's Sorry Now." Everybody would be whistling something on the way out.

Orchestra leaders and musicians were stars, adored by the young people who gathered in front of the orchestra shell, pushing for a closer view. Lewis Philip Hall remem-

Lumina had everything — including motion pictures in the ocean, shown on a large screen in the surf. Viewers in the tiered seats saw a silent movie with the ocean waves beyond. If the tide was out, another large audience — sitting on the sand beneath the veranda — saw the movies for free. Ocean movies eventually ended with the advent of "talkies," which could not be heard above the surf.

NEW HANOVER PUBLIC LIBRARY, LOUIS T. MOORE COLLECTION

bered, "Hanging from the ballroom ceiling, in those years, was a huge globe completely covered with tiny mirrors, and when the beautiful strains of a waltz, such as 'The Sweetheart of Sigma Chi' emerged from the orchestra, the lights were lowered and a spotlight was thrown on the revolving ball, then every young man found his best girl. The huge and shining dance floor then became a dreamy place of slowly swaying bodies—each couple wrapped and lost in their own romantic world."

Intermissions, frequently inserted, gave the dancers an opportunity to buy soft drinks. Some were enhanced, though this was the supposedly alcohol-free Prohibition era. "During intermission," Hall wrote, "numerous groups of people could be seen on the boardwalk, beyond the bright lights, where with paper cups in hand, they stood while one member of the group poured a small amount of liquid in each cup from a pint bottle, or a half gallon fruit jar."

Though Lumina patrons were held to the highest decorum, occasional alcohol use was an open secret. Susan Taylor Block, in *Wilmington through the lens of Louis T. Moore*, wrote that patrons hid their flasks or Mason jars in the sand beneath Lumina: "Wrightsville Beach teenagers raided the jars one night, substituting tea for bourbon. They waited in the shadows and watched gleefully as gentlemen spewed and cursed."

Lumina was now the island's headliner, but it was hardly the only addition to the Wrightsville Beach skyline.

The Hanover Seaside Club, formed in Carolina Beach, opened its second clubhouse on Wrightsville in 1906. The large three-story building with expansive verandas was bigger when it opened than anything on the beach except the Seashore and Tarrymoore hotels. It held a ballroom, dining rooms, a kitchen, a large card room, 14 bedrooms, 60 bath and dressing rooms for beachgoers, and a two-lane bowling alley. Smaller but impressive structures like the eight-bedroom Tar Heelia Inn, built in 1910 with a large wraparound porch, also appeared.

In 1907, Episcopal and Presbyterian churches in Wilmington combined resources and built a small church near Station Two of the trolley line. Though expanded and relocated, the Little Chapel on the Boardwalk continues today.

Harbor Island got in on the act. In 1916, the Tide Water Power Company built a convention center with a 2,000-seat auditorium on the site of the old Island Beach Hotel. It became a major convention site before being converted into a movie theater in 1934 and eventually being torn down. Hugh MacRae's power company now owned the trolley line, Lumina, the Oceanic, and the Harbor Island Pavilion, making it a utility and entertainment juggernaut. In 1917, MacRae announced the sale of his interest to a Pennsylvania utility company.

There was always something to do at Wrightsville. In 1915 and 1916, the Feast of the Lanterns took place, drawing thousands for parades, the crowning of queens, canoe races, fireworks, boat parades, and the like. In 1927 and 1928, Wrightsville shared the Feast of the Pirates with Wilmington. Wrightsville's festivities included fireworks, a grand ball at Lumina, and regattas, boardwalk parades, aquatic events, and beauty contests, all in front of the Oceanic.

Sometimes, the island's attractions were coincidental. An early hydroplane dropped in for a refueling stop on its way to Palm Beach, Florida, in January 1917. It landed in Banks Channel behind the island and stayed for 10 minutes. "Those persons who were fortunate enough to be at the beach were treated to a sight they will not soon forget," the *Wilmington Dispatch* reported the next day. "The big mechanical bird ar-

An early hydroplane drops in for re-fueling in 1917. "Those persons who were fortunate enough to be at the beach were treated to a sight they will not soon forget," the WILMINGTON DISPATCH reported the next day.

NEW HANOVER PUBLIC LIBRARY, ROBERT M. FALES COLLECTION

rived off the beach at 3:55 o'clock and after circling slowly overhead, descended gracefully and glided smoothly across the bosom of the channel."

It was big news, too, when a beach car derailed in May 1918. The trolley went off the track as it was crossing the trestle and fell into the marsh. No one was hurt, at least not seriously, but the accident received widespread publicity.

Growth continued. St. Mary's Star of the Sea, a chapel built about 1912 or 1913, was served by Catholic priests, mostly from Wilmington. Another noteworthy newcomer was Roberts Market, which continues today as the oldest business on the island. Rupert Benson explained how it got started: "Mr. C. S. Roberts, sick, came to the beach in 1919 to get well and liked it so much, he just forgot to leave."

The first crown jewel of the island, the Seashore Hotel, continued to light up the oceanfront, now more literally. On July 1, 1910, just in time for the record-breaking Fourth, the hotel formally opened its Steel Pier. Made solely of steel like the famed Steel Pier in Atlantic City, it was said to be the only one of its kind on the south Atlantic coast. The Seashore lighted its 700-foot reach out into the Atlantic Ocean, all the way to the two-story pavilion and observation deck at the end. The way it illuminated the incoming waves drew raves from visitors, no easy feat with Lumina nearby.

The charmed life of the original Seashore, however, came to a burning end after two decades on the night of June 26, 1919. Fire, like storms, was always a problem on the beach. On the night of its demise, the Seashore was full with more than 400 guests, many of whom were on the broad porches. Others were strolling the brightly illuminated pier. About 10:25, chaos broke out with cries of "Fire!"

Employees with fire extinguishers ran to the third floor. Guests rushed to get their belongings and flee the building. Flames spread rapidly. A bucket brigade was formed, its long lines extending to Banks Channel. Employees, guests, island residents, and visitors joined the lines, passing full buckets of water to the Seashore and empty ones back. The crowded Lumina emptied, and its patrons, who had been dancing moments before, joined in.

The bucket brigade was further newsworthy for the presence of an unlikely gown- and jewel-bedecked fire woman, one of the wealthiest people in America. The next day's *Wilmington Dispatch* had the story under the headline, "Seventy Million Dollar Heiress in Bucket Brigade." It read in part,

> One lone link in the chain of bucket passers is worth a cool seventy million dollars. This introduces Mrs. Lawrence Wise Lewis, chief beneficiary of the late Mrs. Robert Worth Bingham, second widow of Henry M. Flagler, Standard Oil multi-millionaire.

Mrs. Lewis worked tirelessly with the other members of the volunteer brigade until the heat from the building forced discontinuance of their efforts.

The fact that the Northrop cottage was saved was due in a measure to the efforts of Mrs. Lewis who could easily repair all damage done with her own money. It was her desire to help that prompted her and not because she once thought of the monetary value of the property.

The evening gown she wore was forgotten and not a thought was given to the jewels that adorned her hands as she labored more conscientiously than any hod carrier in her efforts to prevent further destruction.

The Seashore Hotel added a premier attraction in 1910, the Steel Pier, which featured a two-story pavilion at the end. The pier was brilliantly illuminated at night, drawing raves even from guests of Lumina, the ultimate house of lights.

AUTHOR COLLECTION

The bucket brigade was of minimal effectiveness in saving the Seashore. The building fueled the fire, and a stiff wind from the northwest fanned it. There was little chance. Flames were leaping 200 feet into the air. The sky was lit up for miles. The Wilmington Fire Department loaded an engine onto a power-company freight car for the trip to the beach but arrived too late to be of use. Worse, word reached Wilmington that the entire beach was aflame. Panicked and curious city dwellers hopped in their cars and clogged the Shell Road, chasing the red glare in the sky.

Thanks to a wind shift, nearby Lumina was spared.

The Seashore was quickly consumed. Hotel guests filled the beach, alongside luggage and furniture. All 400-plus escaped, and most had their belongings. They stood and watched the crackling, roaring inferno take the hotel. The fire would be traced to defective wiring in the third-floor walls, the damage estimated at $150,000. Only $60,000 was covered by insurance.

The Steel Pier was undamaged. Even that blessing, however, was short-lived. A little over one year later, in September 1920, a series of storms severely damaged the pier. Just four months after that, on January 27, 1921, a ferocious winter storm from the northeast ripped free the remaining part of the pier and carried it south along the beach. It later crashed into the foundation pilings of a cottage, toppling it like a house of cards.

In 1922, the Seashore Hotel was rebuilt on the southern end of the old site, though without a pier. The three-story replacement had 60 rooms with baths. The first floor included a spacious lobby and a large dining room.

Meanwhile, in 1925, the Channel View Hotel was built on the ocean side of the tracks at Station One, the first stop for visitors to the island. Pop Gray's Soda Shop took up half the first floor and became a popular stop, especially for after-Lumina guests at night. Across the tracks was Bud Werkheiser's Stand—later to become the site of Newell's, then still later of Wings—which sold newspapers, souvenirs, and the like. With the Oceanic Hotel nearby, Station One became a beehive of summertime activity, especially on Friday and Saturday evenings. Arriving guests and black porters milled with fun seekers and sometimes an impromptu but talented band, the Snow Birds.

Even off the island, building was afoot. In 1920, Dr. James Buren Sidbury opened the famed Babies Hospital nearby on the mainland at Wrightsville Sound. Though it burned to the ground in 1927, it was replaced with a brick building nearby that stood for more than three-quarters of a century.

The Roaring '20s were a time of excitement and energy in America. Wrightsville, already a place of excitement and energy, was primed to capitalize. Yet much of its allure remained its secluded location, its identity as a place where the outside world rarely seemed to intrude. Lewis Philip Hall, if given to occasional hyperbole, captured the spirit in his 1975 book:

> Wrightsville Beach in this era was a secluded island where genteel people vacationed and lived summer after summer. Without a doubt, it was different from any other resort anywhere or in any era.
>
> Isolated from the noise and frustrations of the city by a mile wide expanse of tidal marsh grass and winding channels stretching away to the north and south as far as the eye could see; bordered on the east by the roaring surf of the broad Atlantic Ocean; its only connection with the busy world was the half mile long railway trestle—it was a wonderful refuge.

Its flaming sunsets, tinting the clouds in delicate shades of orange, lavender, and grays as viewed across the wide expanse of salt marsh; the quiet breath-taking magnificence of a deep yellow moon rising seemingly out of the depths of a heaving ocean; or even the jagged bolts of lightning flashing from one black cloud bank to another, or into the sea—was like a tonic that calmed the nerves and lifted the spirits.

The small, isolated island was changing, however. In 1926, MacRae extended it, pushing Moore's Inlet farther north by filling in from Asheville Street to Salisbury Street. This northern extension was created by putting up a bulkhead and filling behind it with sand. It was the first of several beach enlargements.

Likewise, in 1925, the Hammocks was enlarged to create what would become Shore Acres Island and later Harbor Island. In 1926, the Shore Acres development of homes was begun here on lots sold by the Tide Water Power Company. A newspaper at the time said, "There will always be those

An aerial shot from the 1920s shows how much Wrightsville Beach had grown. The Atlantic Ocean is to the left and Banks Channel to the right. The boardwalk runs the length of the island. The trolley tracks are immediately to the right of it.
NEW HANOVER PUBLIC LIBRARY, LOUIS T. MOORE COLLECTION

A postcard from the late 1920s highlights the foot bridge and trolley tracks to the outer island from Shore Acres Island, the name given the Hammocks after the opening of the Shore Acres development of homes. Boaters and the Oceanic Hotel are in the background. Later, the interior island would become Harbor Island.

AUTHOR COLLECTION

who prefer this beach because of the fact that no motor cars will ever disturb the quietude." The following year, the power company began selling individual lots on the outer beach island as well.

In 1926, too, the Wilmington–Wrightsville Beach Causeway was built from the mainland at Wrightsville Sound to Harbor Island. The $138,000 causeway, constructed by a Florida firm, A. E. Fitkin, cost 10 cents to traverse. "Thanks to the dredge, *Caulkins Territory*, an area long sacred to the electric train has been opened to the motor car," the *Morning Star* noted.

Now, for the first time, automobiles could come within a stone's throw of the beach.

Chapter Seven

SHELL ISLAND AND A SEPARATE PARADISE

Shell Island was an uninhabited outpost of sand dunes and sea oats, a land of beauty known as a magnet for shell seekers and excursionists.

In the years before World War I, the Oceanic Hotel ran excursions for its guests aboard two sailboats—a 60-footer that could carry 50 or 60 people and a smaller craft that could carry 35. The most popular of these excursions were across Moore's Inlet to Shell Island, just to the north. Sometimes called Moore's Beach, it was a place of striking natural beauty. Lewis Philip Hall described its inhabitants: "The broad shore of Shell Island was covered with thousands of sea shells, at that time, and it was also the home of myriads of sea fowl, that built their nests here and raised their young among the high dunes of this un-inhabited and quiet place."

The island was for a time in 1910 the site where two men worked in secret on developing an airplane. Word was out that H. M. Chase, manager of a chemical company, and J. F. Gouverneur, vice president of the Tide Water Power Company, would fly a plane on July 4 at Wrightsville. Five thousand turned out to the island that day. No flight was made, no word appeared in the papers that had promoted it, and many thought it had been a trick to lure more to the beach via Tide Water's beach cars.

Regardless, the Shell Island–developed plane was indeed flown, though several months later and for but a single flight. The flight would qualify as brief. A Wilmington paper reported on November 15, 1910, that Chase had flown at Wrightsville the previous day—the first flight in North Carolina since the Wright brothers had made their return to Kitty Hawk in 1908. "When the tide had receded sufficiently," the paper said, "the aeroplane was run along the beach for some distance until it gradually rose in flight to a height of about five feet and continued for some distance, just enough to demonstrate its ability to fly." It apparently never flew again because the weight of the motor prevented long flights. The event passed into history.

That was the last time most heard of Shell Island until 1923, when plans were developed for a $75,000 "Negro resort."

In the era of segregation, African-Americans were kept from most things of value, and ocean resorts were certainly among them. A bathhouse and a small pavilion for blacks had been built in the late 1800s at Ocean View Beach. A larger 30-by-50-foot pavilion was constructed for blacks in the early 20th century and operated at least until 1907. But there was little more. Blacks later were allowed in the ocean only at the little-used northern extension. Anne Russell, in *The Carolina Yacht Club Chronicles*, wrote of a typical situation in the 1920s, a black maid watching a white family's children on the more popular beach: "The children were not allowed to venture very far out into the water, for Pearl's supervision ended at the tide's edge."

In 1917, blacks petitioned the Tide Water Power Company to set apart the extreme southern part of Wrightsville

Few ventured onto Shell Island, a beautiful but remote spot, before the 1920s. "The broad shore of Shell Island was covered with thousands of sea shells, at that time," Lewis Philip Hall wrote, "and it was also the home of myriads of sea fowl, that built their nests here and raised their young among the high dunes of this un-inhabited and quiet place." Among those who did were sailboat excursionists from the Oceanic Hotel. At the right is the pavilion where the boats were kept.

NEW HANOVER PUBLIC LIBRARY, LOUIS T. MOORE COLLECTION

Beach for a blacks-only pavilion and beach. A number of prominent whites endorsed the petition, including Mayors Thomas H. Wright of Wrightsville Beach and P. Q. Moore of Wilmington. But white residents counter-petitioned, saying that allowing blacks a place at the beach would "tend to destroy property values" and "lead to racial disturbances." The idea dropped from the news pages.

But by 1923, C. B. Parmele and Wright, president and vice president of the Home Realty Company, bought Shell Island. The two had been among the whites to petition for a Wrightsville spot. Now, they began work on a large pavilion, bathhouses, restaurants, drinks stands, piers, systems for electric lights and sewers, and a well for drinking water. Black professionals were building private cottages as well.

An April 16, 1923, edition of the *Wilmington Star* said the $15,000 pavilion was nearing completion. It would include "a spacious veranda, similar to the one at Lumina, from which the patrons of the pavilion might sit evenings and view motion pictures." Tide Water Power was extending its track on Harbor Island. Stone Towing would operate a ferry from Harbor Island to Shell Island.

Even this separate island was alarming to some whites. An editorial in the May 26, 1923, *Wilmington News* entitled "Wrightsville Still White" wanted to assuage the fears of segregationists who had heard rumors Wrightsville Beach would be admitting blacks:

> An impression has gone abroad from Wilmington, so we are reliably informed that Wrightsville Beach has been opened to negroes, the sole basis of course being the announcement that a resort for negroes was to be opened this summer on Shell Island, across the inlet from Wrightsville Beach. Now credulous persons in the upper end of the state are beginning to talk of other resorts for their summer vacation.
>
> As a matter of fact, the establishing of a negro resort at Shell Island will have no effect whatsoever on Wrightsville Beach, separated as it is by the width of the inlet from the new playground. To the skeptics and the doubters, and those who have given ear to this preposterous rumor let us say that racial lines are still observed at Wrightsville Beach, and that the waters of the Atlantic ocean still beat against her borders on all sides, divorcing it completely, entirely and eternally from those fictitious drawbacks which the fertile imagery of Dame Rumor has woven.

"The National Negro Playground" was an answer to "the Playground of the South" just across Moore's Inlet at Wrightsville. There was certainly a demand. Large crowds swarmed Shell Island Beach, first taking the train to Harbor

Island, then one of four daily round trips across to the beach in a gasoline-powered ferry. The Tide Water Power Company, seeing the potential, made plans to extend a beach trolley line from Harbor Island. Though most visitors were from Wilmington, black beachgoers came from as far away as New York and Alabama, and even several foreign countries. The Negro Elks, holding their state convention in Wilmington in 1926, chose Shell Island as the site of the annual ball.

Frank W. Avant, an African-American doctor, was Shell Island's principal organizer. He lined up jazz performances from the likes of Lindsey Brown, "North Carolina's greatest tenor," and John Cabbage Walter.

"The National Negro Playground" occupied Shell Island for part of the 1920s. Afterward, the island was largely ignored again until the mid-1960s, when an inlet separating it from Wrightsville Beach was closed. Developers rushed to the new land. Among the most imposing structures was the Shell Island Resort. Marshlands still separate it from the Intracoastal Waterway and the mainland.

PHOTOGRAPH BY VICKI McALLISTER

But the beach was the draw. Avant, quoted in the June 1, 1924, *Morning Star*, said, "Shell Island, the premier Negro resort of America, with its two miles of ocean front, spreads itself out like some fairyland along the mighty water. The distinctive feature in connection with Shell Island is the erection of private cottages along the beach front by individuals of our race, which afford every comfort, leisure and privacy."

Greg Watkins, writing in the 1997 *Wrightsville Beach: A Pictorial History*, told the story of one man who visited the island as a child:

> Lewis Williams recalls that when he was a young lad on summer Sundays at 8 A.M., he and his brother Lawrence and their mother, Lillian Pierce Williams, would arrive at 13th and Ann Streets in downtown Wilmington and board a "special" beach car bound for sun and surf at Shell Island. At the big powerhouse station on Wrightsville Sound, they crossed a narrow trestle to the Harbor Island Causeway. Just before reaching the trestle at Banks Channel, the beach cars turned sharply to the left and ran to the northern extension of Harbor Island. At the end of the spur, beachgoers awaited the arrival of the small ferry to transport them across Moore's Inlet to Shell Island. The ferry was long and light in color with seats on one side, open above the gunwales, and covered by a canvas top. A concession stand near the center of the boat sold popcorn, cotton candy, and colored pinwheels which hummed in the breeze. Although Lewis was afraid of the water, he was always excited to go to the beach. While other boys made a bee-line for the breakers, Lewis was content to build sand castles and listen to the music from Shell Island Pavilion.

"There was never any trouble on those trips to Shell Island. Everyone was pleasant and orderly. It was good clean fun, a time I will always remember," Williams recalls.

The end came unceremoniously. Shell Island was abandoned in 1926, just three years after its start, seemingly with little public notice. The island may have been too successful or otherwise angered whites. Lewis Philip Hall explained, "After a series of fires, of undetermined origin, which destroyed a number of public buildings, the island was abandoned by man and left to the shy and fragile, silver and cream ghost crabs that tip-toe across the crystal sands of the first National Negro resort."

The island would not see development again for four decades, following the merging of Shell Island into what would become a longer Wrightsville Beach island. The National Negro Playground faded into memory.

Chapter Eight

TROUBLE WASHES ASHORE

It may have been M. M. Riley, Jr., an agent of the Clyde Line Steamship Company, who saw it first, sitting there practically in his front yard as he went out for his daily pre-breakfast walk. Or it may have been his young son, Roger, who saw it and came running in to tell his mother: "Hey, Mama, the porpoises are pushing a big fish up on the beach. Come look! Come look!"

The story is told both ways, and other ways as well, but what is certain is that on Thursday morning, April 5, 1928, an enormous intruder lay in the surf practically in the Rileys' front yard. This was no big fish. This was an adult whale, beached and dead.

Whales were once plentiful along the North Carolina coast, particularly off the Outer Banks, and their oil provided seamen with a good living. But whalers steadily thinned the population until North Carolina whales became an anomaly. The last one was killed off Carteret County in 1898.

Now, here was another, lying dead in the surf.

News of the Rileys' discovery quickly spread to Wilmington. Few people lived on the beach, particularly in April. But within hours, cars were bumper to bumper on the newly built causeway to Harbor Island. As the *Wilmington Star* reported the next morning, "Crowds began flocking to the beach, in picnic swarms, throughout the day, the roads being virtually a processional of autos, the streets loaded to capacity."

The beach trolley cars were equally busy hauling sight-seers. Indeed, Lewis Philip Hall, in *Land of the Golden River*, wrote, "The private lawn, the flower garden, and even the front porch of the cottage of Mrs. Riley, on the northern end of the island, became 'public property' as strangers tramped back and forth across her yard. All her pleas and her de-mands to disperse were ignored as the crowd milled about, seeking a better position from which to view the mammal. It was later estimated that at least 50,000 people from a half dozen states visited the site."

No wonder. The male sperm whale was estimated to weigh more than 100,000 pounds, an almost unheard-of 50 to 55 tons, making it the largest of the species ever found in these waters. (It was not quite so massive, however, as some enthusiastic news reports had it. Estimates grew to as much as 150 tons. Even two years later, one newspaper placed the weight at 95 tons.) The whale would prove to be 54 feet, two inches in length, with a girth of 33 feet. Its tail alone was 14 feet wide. Its lower jaw, 10 feet long, contained 46 teeth that fit into sockets in the upper jaw, which had no teeth.

Why it had journeyed to Wrightsville was a mystery. One theory was that it may have been accompanying a sick female overtaken by an odd illness, one that caused females to swim in a direct line until either overcoming the illness or beaching themselves. Their male mates remained until they recovered or died.

Years later, in 1992, a much smaller and younger sperm whale would wash ashore at Wrightsville and soon die in the surf. The stomach of that 28-foot female proved to be full

A 54-foot-long adult male sperm whale washed up on Wrightsville Beach in 1928. More than 50,000 people came to see it over the next two weeks, even though there was no automobile access to the island, and visitors had to ride a beach trolley or walk across two lengthy footbridges. More than 15,000 visited on Easter Sunday.

N.C. MUSEUM OF NATURAL SCIENCES

of marine trash it had eaten: 30 feet of nylon rope, a plastic gallon bleach bottle, a plastic bag, a large blob of raw latex, and a fishing float. Veterinarians believed it starved to death because it couldn't squeeze in enough real food. In contrast to the wild events of 1928, that small whale's appearance created only a ripple of attention.

It is hard to exaggerate the interest in April 1928. The beached whale immediately became Wrightsville's largest tourist attraction by far. Later newspaper accounts would say that it "drew heavier than any other event in the history of Wilmington" as well.

It also created Wrightsville's largest problem. The April 6 *Star* hinted at the issue to come: "Incidentally, the appearance of the carcass and its huge volume has created a sanitary problem." The county health official, Dr. John H. Hamilton, was to confer with Wrightsville officials and a local debris-removal contractor about the whale. "It will be removed before it becomes a menace to health," the article ended hopefully.

But where would it go? A fertilizer factory said no thanks. Mayor George E. Kidder offered the rotting carcass to the North Carolina State Museum in Raleigh. The offer was initially rejected, museum director H. H. Brimley wrote later, as "said offer included the removal of the body from the beach, an expensive operation." The following Sunday, associate curator Harry T. Davis did go to the island and "cut off the projecting part of the lower jaw as a material record of the incident, and went home to weep over what we had lost," Brimley wrote.

Meanwhile, the county board of health had ordered the town to tow the thing 25 miles out to sea and release it.

By now, the whale was, quite simply, an enormous news story, an enormous tourist attraction, and an enormous headache. The rotting carcass smelled. Photographers and newsreel cameramen arrived. The crowds grew. A retrospective piece 35 years later in *The State* magazine described the mad scene: "Easter Sunday, April 8, came and with it crowds began to flock into the area to see the big fish. Fifteen thousand people thronged and milled over the sands to get a glimpse of the great creature. The multitudes began arriving at 4:30 in the morning. All the restaurants in Wilmington and Wrightsville Beach stayed open through the night to serve the jostling mass of humanity. Traffic was jammed, and some drivers abandoned their vehicles on the side of the road when the bumper-to-bumper flow of autos bogged down."

The masses overran the island, swarming porches on the cottages with the best views and literally tearing them from the houses. They overran lawns, flower gardens, and picket fences. No one fared worse than the Rileys. Helen Riley, responding later to a newspaper letter from an oil distributor who had cheered the newfound dollars, countered that the mobs had nearly driven the family from its home. Three times her house caught fire from cigarettes tossed underneath, she wrote. Two windows were broken, her boardwalk was wrecked, and a new, expensive flower garden was destroyed.

Robert Martin Fales, author of *Wilmington Yesteryear*, was a freshman at Wake Forest College. "In April 1928 it was something of a distinction to hail from Wilmington," he wrote, "since every newspaper in the state headlined the big story that an enormous whale had washed ashore on the northern extension of Wrightsville Beach." When the weekend came, he and his roommates signed out of the dormitory and headed as quickly as they could to Wrightsville. That's when Fales heard yet another version of the story:

> We didn't have to be in town very long before we heard the story that everyone was repeating—that of the whale's initial discovery.
>
> At that time it was well known to the residents of Wrightsville Beach that the old man who lived in the cottage on the northern end of the island had become a chronic drunkard who drank day and night. His credibility had been destroyed by drinking, and his disgusted wife had moved into her own bedroom. While the couple slept, the whale washed ashore. In the morning, the old man woke up, went to the bathroom, and then made his way to the kitchen for his customary stiff first drink. He then went out to the porch to pick up the *Morning Star*, looked out to sea, and spotted the beached whale. Running into his wife's bedroom, he shook her until she roused and shouted over and over, "Mary, Mary, get up! There's a great big

whale in front of the house!!!" His wife rolled over grumbling, "Go get in bed, you drunk S.O.B. You are simply seeing things again."

That may have been the only humor in the situation. Moving the whale was a chore. Nothing could be done in the face of a three-day strong wind that blew in Easter night. The storm actually moved the whale carcass up the beach and also deposited the remaining portion of its massive, 600-pound lower jaw . . . somewhere. The jaw may have been buried in the sand. It may have been swept out to sea. Either way, it was gone.

By Wednesday, April 11, the continuing stench of the sun-baked whale had thinned the crowds considerably. By

The sheer size of the 50-ton-plus whale, combined with storms and bad weather days, made its removal difficult. To make matters worse, its carcass began rotting, emitting a huge stench. The whale quickly earned the nickname "Trouble." Officially, the whale was named "Wrightsville" — but "Trouble" stuck, nonetheless.

N.C. MUSEUM OF NATURAL SCIENCES

now, the townspeople had given the whale an apt name: Trouble. Actually, it officially had a different name, says assistant librarian and archivist Margaret Cotrufo of what is now the North Carolina Museum of Natural Sciences. "Davis named it Wrightsville, but nobody knows that," Cotrufo says. "Brimley announced it on the radio."

But Trouble it was. Trouble, indeed. The county health officer, Dr. Hamilton, already had threatened to "throw the book" at Wrightsville officials "if something isn't done immediately."

It's not that they weren't trying. The Stone Towing Company, whose work normally included towing the large steamships coming into the port of Wilmington, was hired to remove Trouble. It wrapped a heavy towline around the whale's carcass, sans the missing lower jaw, part of which Davis had removed on Easter. But a vicious nor'easter blew in, and the seas were rough—too rough for tugboats to get near. Even when the seas abated, the two tugboats were not up to the task. The whale was held firmly by the sucking sands, and the tugs retreated.

They returned on Friday, April 12, this time staying at anchor 1,500 feet offshore. Meanwhile, the salvage crew, with help from the Coast Guard at Oak Island (according to one account) or a corps of convicts (according to another), tunneled beneath the carcass, getting enough space to wrap a heavy cable eight times around it. The line was attached to the tugs, which pulled for an hour from offshore. Finally, they pulled Trouble from the sands, rolling him over once. From that point, each pull of the tugboats rolled the whale nearer the water. Eventually, the carcass reached the sea and floated.

State officials had ordered the town to "tow the whale twenty-five miles out to sea and there set it adrift." But museum curator Brimley and associate curator Davis had the orders changed to the following: "Tow the whale twenty miles up the coast and there set it adrift." So Trouble was hauled twenty miles up to the largely uninhabited Topsail Island, then known as Topsail Beach. There, a friend of Brimley's, Theodore Empire, owned a mile of desolate beach property near Topsail Inlet.

Trouble was still trouble.

The museum hired a local gasoline-boat owner, Captain Ramp Smith, to bring the whale ashore. But once the whale reached Topsail and was released, the tide was falling. A southeast wind was blowing hard, too, pushing Smith's boat near the shore. Moreover, heavy chains had been left around the small of the whale's tail, weighing it down. Both boat and whale drifted dangerously toward the breakers, and the boat was taking on water. A 110-foot sub-chaser-type Coast Guard cutter came racing to the scene.

The ship was not there to help, at least not initially. This being Prohibition, the Coast Guard was using navy destroyers to help fight the illegal rum-running traffic; Caribbean ships were known to stash rum on the beaches for later pickup. "The officer of the government boat, thinking our crew were at work dragging for a cache of liquor, shifted his helm and brought his boat tearing up," Brimley wrote, "but on finding our men engaged in the perfectly legitimate operation of trying to salvage a very-much-spoiled sperm whale, he offered his assistance."

Even with the cutter and a favorable wind, however, it would be five hours before the whale was finally grounded on a shoal at Topsail.

Travails continued. Sometime during the night, someone removed the lines holding Trouble on the beach. He went adrift, though fortunately he hung up on a shoal. There in the surf, a nine-foot-tall platform had to be built. Davis and laborers began stripping large chunks of blubber and flesh from Trouble's frame and throwing them into the sea. Thousands of sea gulls and other birds flocked to the feast. At night, ghost crabs continued the work.

Topsail was an island for fishing, though, and not everyone was thrilled by the intruder. Complaining letters were sent to the museum, health officials, congressmen, and even the governor. One unsigned letter released to the press complained about "parking a uzed [sic] whale. . . . It's poor policy to deposit your trash in your neighbor's back yard." Some seemed more mercenary, offering to come up with the missing whale jaw for a price. One man wanted $20 per day for spoiled fishing. "The fishermen have said that their fishing was ruined for days by the foul flesh," noted the *Wilmington Morning Star* in a long front-page retrospective eight months later, "but most game fish do not take account of the condition of the flesh, so there is some question about any bills they may present ever being paid."

Nearly a dozen barrels of oil and spermaceti were poured into the water, too, where the spermaceti solidified into white flakes. Davis recalled the immense project: "We used broad axes and bush axes. Then we took the bones and buried them in the sand on the beach so the sand crabs could eat the remaining flesh." The expectation was that the oil would leak from the bones. By April 29, the bones were buried in a 15-by-39-foot grave.

Not until September did Davis return to Topsail for an inspection. He announced then that the bones could be reassembled in the museum in Raleigh by late fall.

So, in December, the four tons of bones—some 15 feet long and requiring several men to carry them—were dug up and transported in three boats nearly two miles to solid land. The plan was to move the bones to two large highway-department trucks for the 175-mile trip to Raleigh. But nothing about Trouble was easy. One of the trucks became stuck and had to be pulled from the sand. "They had to wait while Davis went to Wilmington for a chain," Cotrufo says. "Then it broke. They had to go back to Wilmington for another chain."

Even in Raleigh, Trouble was a chore. Burial on Topsail had left the bones fairly clean. But masses of fibrous tissue remained on them, so they couldn't be placed on the platform that had been built in the court of the museum. The bones, in essence, needed to be reburied. They were taken to the highway department's "truck patch" adjoining the state fairgrounds and buried above ground in a large sand-filled box for 10 months. It would have been longer, Brimley noted, except the ground needed to be cleared for the 1929 North

Trouble today hangs from the ceiling of what is now the North Carolina Museum of Natural Sciences. The whale is the museum's headliner and a stylized version of Trouble is even incorporated into the museum's logo.

MARGARET COTRUFO, N.C. MUSEUM OF NATURAL SCIENCES

Carolina State Fair. The bones next were taken to the roof of the state office heating plant, the final step in the curing process. With winter nearing, they were brought inside the museum, where they were scrubbed with lye and ammonia.

Trouble still needed a lower jaw. Brimley found one in the personal collection of Dr. Robert Cushman Murphy, a curator at the American Museum of Natural History, and the museum bought it for $40. Artificial teeth were made as well.

The long task of reassembling the skeleton began. Even then, Trouble lived up to his name. No floor space at the museum was large enough to display him. Brimley and an engineer creatively solved the problem by suspending the 55-foot skeleton from the second-floor rafters. It was worth the effort. Brimley later called it "the most outstanding and valuable individual specimen the Museum has ever secured."

Trouble has since been taken down twice—once for renovations and once for cleaning in preparation for the museum's new building. His is one of five whale skeletons hanging in the entrance to the Coastal North Carolina Gallery of the Museum of Natural Sciences. Trouble is the headliner. Generations of children, brought by parents and by schools, have oohed and aahed. Even adults join the adulation.

The whale has become so iconic an image and so associated with the museum, in fact, that a stylized image of him in life is now its logo. Museum merchandise—T-shirts, mugs, magnets, patches, key chains—all feature the famous sperm whale that landed on Wrightsville Beach so many years ago.

At long last, Trouble is anything but.

Chapter Nine

THE GREAT FIRE OF 1934

"On Sunday afternoon, January 28, 1934," wrote Rupert Benson in his *Historical Narrative 1841–1972 of Wrightsville Beach, North Carolina*, "a great billow of smoke and fire arose from the peaceful Kitty Cottage by the Sea, and Wrightsville Beach was shocked out of its care free mind."

The Kitty Cottage was a large summer boardinghouse on the beach operated by Mrs. John A. Snyder. The Kitty apparently had taken its name from its busy poker tables or, according to another version, had actually *given* its name to the pots of money used in those games. Regardless, at 12:30 P.M., smoke rose from the cottage. Edmund Rogers, strolling the boardwalk near Station Two, saw it first. Rogers and friends opened the door.

The interior was a mass of flames.

The Wilmington Fire Department was summoned. But the wind was already lifting sparks, burning embers, and black smoke into the air. Soon, the neighboring Carolina Cottage and its dining rooms were on fire. So, too, were the Parlsey Boardinghouse and the Sternberger Cottages. The Sigmund Bear, Thomas H. Wright, and Alexander Sprunt homes were soon aflame. The fire department arrived. But

The Fire of 1934 started in the Kitty Cottage boardinghouse. "One story is that it was one of the poker player's cigarettes," says Bill Creasy, who as a boy watched his family's home be destroyed. "Another is that it was somehow started by someone ironing upstairs. But they don't know."

AUTHOR COLLECTION

the wind, which had been from the west, now began blowing from the south, and with more intensity. The bucket brigade and the wheel-cart fire engine had no chance against the roaring flames, fanned by gale-force winds. The firefighters and a large number of volunteers could only watch.

Sparks began to leap from building to building. Embers were carried along and dropped on the roof of the Oceanic Hotel. That famous old hotel soon was an inferno.

So was nearly everything else on the northern third of the island. The fire rolled over more than a hundred buildings, swallowing cottages, inns, and boardwalks. Streetcar rails were twisted by the intense heat. Sand fleas were baked alive.

Bill Creasy still remembers the fire vividly, though he was but six years old at the time. His family lived in Wilmington and spent its summers at Wrightsville. "That was January 28, 1934," Creasy remembers now, sitting in his home just blocks away. "My father got a call that the beach was on fire. He said, 'Come on. Let's go see what we could see.'" The Creasys drove over but were stopped at the bridge.

"We stood over there and watched the whole beach burn," he says. "It was an image burned in my mind. . . . It took about three hours to burn." There was no fire department on the island. The wind was up. The fire hopped from building to building. "It was so hot that burning embers would rise up and drop on the roof of the next one." The big loss, of course, was the mammoth Oceanic.

A few buildings here and there at the north end somehow were missed. "My grandmother ran the Edgewater Hotel—what it was was a boardinghouse with 20 to 25 rooms—and it did not burn," Creasy says.

The big mystery was how the fire started in the Kitty Cottage. "One story is that it was one of the poker player's cigarettes," says Creasy, recognized as an island historian. "Another is that it was somehow started by someone ironing upstairs. But they don't know."

The fire could have been even worse, according to Benson: "It is said the towering Sand Dunes off the Ewing Cottage on the north, shut off flames and served as a wind funnel, diverting the flying embers. [F]ive cottages to the north were saved and on West Columbia St., the Edgewater Cottage and two residences owned by Mr. Frinklestein and Mr. Warshauer were saved by the efforts of a bucket brigade and a garden hose." Otherwise, ashes were everywhere. The devastation was virtually complete from Station Two north, so much so that it was far easier to count the cottages left standing than those that had been destroyed.

Fire has always been the most unpredictable of beach threats, nearly as dangerous as hurricanes. Wooden structures, high winds, and a distant fire department made an uncomfortable combination. Few beach communities have been spared serious fires. Wrightsville Beach has had more than its share.

The Seashore Hotel fire of 1919 brought headlines, but there were many others. Periodically, newspaper accounts reported another cottage had burned to the ground. Some fires were more threatening. In 1908, a fire that began in the restaurant of the 35-room Ocean View Hotel destroyed both the hotel and the Casino theater. In 1920, a fire that originated in the Cooleemee Cottage on the northern extension of the island destroyed three cottages, seriously endangered a fourth, and for a time seemed likely to threaten the entire island. Only a bucket brigade of neighbors and staff of the nearby Oceanic Hotel limited the damage. In 1948, a

Driven by wind, the fire spread quickly and destroyed most of what was then the northern portion of Wrightsville Beach. More than 103 cottages and other structures were burned to the ground.
NEW HANOVER PUBLIC LIBRARY, LOUIS T. MOORE COLLECTION

fire started in an oil stove, then, fanned by a stiff southeast wind, destroyed five large buildings, partially burned a sixth, and caused smoke damage to a seventh. Lost were the 30-room Atlantic Inn, the six-unit Judy Apartments, and several residences, the total loss estimated at $65,000. A 1981 fire destroyed the Hanover Seaside Club and killed a fireman.

But nothing has approached the breadth of what is re-called as "the Great Fire of 1934."

Lewis Philip Hall described the scene: "Two and one-half hours after the fire was discovered, from the Carolina Cottage north only blackened chimneys, charred embers and thousands of dead sand fleas covered the baked sand dunes. Thousands of dollars worth of furnishings and other prop-erty that was removed from the structures later burned as the fire crept over the boardwalks and through the dry sea grass which carpeted the sand. The furniture spread along the ocean beach and the banks of the sound was washed into the water by the rising tide. A dozen or more house cats, with singed whiskers, roamed through the desolate scene, appar-ently looking for their homes among the smoking ruins."

When the damage was calculated, at least 103 buildings had been destroyed. Among them were 92 cottages, as well as the 103-room Oceanic Hotel, The Landis, Chandler Ocean Inn, and three of the largest boardinghouses—the Kitty Cot-tage, the Carolina Cottage, and the Parsley. So, too, was Rob-erts Market.

Interestingly, at Station One, the Channel View Hotel and Pop Gray's Soda Shop were not destroyed, but the fire brought business activity to a halt. Pop Gray later opened a drugstore north of the stop. The Tar Heelia Inn on North Lumina Avenue, built in 1910, also survived. And of course, most of the southern two-thirds of the island was left un-harmed, including Lumina.

The *Wilmington Morning Star* emblazoned the tragedy

Oceanic Hotel, Wrightsville Beach, N. C.

The glamorous Oceanic Hotel, valued at $125,000 even in Depression-era dollars, was the major casualty of the 1934 fire. The town's overall loss was estimated at $500,000, a substantial portion of $1.2 million total property value.
AUTHOR COLLECTION

in a banner headline: "Destructive Fire Rakes Wrightsville." A subhead read, "103 Buildings Are Leveled, Including Oceanic Hotel, With Loss of $1,000,000." The $1 million figure would prove an exaggeration; the loss later was estimated at $728,510—the Oceanic alone was valued at $125,000—and finally at $500,000. Any was an astonishing total in Depression-era dollars. In 1933, property in Wrightsville was valued at $1.2 million, brought down by the Depression from its $1.3 million of the preceding five years. That meant the loss from the Great Fire of 1934 was nearly half the town's value.

The psychological loss was as great. Just remembering the Oceanic, Benson wrote wistfully nearly four decades later, "with its dinner music that could be heard for blocks around, the elite and lovely promenade, its vast porches . . .

makes one wish some of this could come back."

Over the ensuing days and weeks, there was talk that the resort town itself was gone for good. Rebuilding the island would be too difficult. Too much had been lost. Indeed, it would be years before the town recovered financially. Worse, Hall wrote, "the results of that inferno cast a pall over the island that failed to disappear for several decades."

Wrightsville had indeed been shocked out of its carefree mind.

The fire is memorialized on this marker for Station Two of the old seven-stop streetcar line. It says: "Beach Car Stop for Kitty Cottage, Origin of the 1934 Fire."
PHOTOGRAPH BY
VICKI McALLISTER

Chapter Ten

EMERGING FROM THE ASHES

Thirty-five years after its first disaster—the Big Storm of 1899—Wrightsville was reeling again.

And then rebuilding again.

Within two weeks of the fire of January 28, 1934, the Tide Water Power Company began repairing its tracks, the Southern Bell Telephone and Telegraph Company replaced lines, and the town of Wrightsville Beach started rebuilding a supply house. The energy level was high. By March, a crew of 37 federal Civil Works Administration (CWA) workers was on site, clearing away debris so boardwalks and three small fire and tool houses could be rebuilt. By April, the main boardwalks on North Lumina and Ocean avenues were replaced. By June, so were three side-street walkways, and 23 buildings were either completed or under way.

Mrs. Snyder remodeled the annex to the now-infamous Kitty Cottage in time to open for the coming season. The Wilmington Light Infantry, too, rebuilt its clubhouse, at the not inconsequential cost of $2,200.

As important as rebuilding was getting the word out. The Wrightsville Beach Board of Aldermen prepared 10,000 leaflets to be passed out across the state, saying Wrightsville was not destroyed. The beach did sustain a considerable loss, the board said, but "there still remain many cottages and hotels that were untouched by fire." The resort would be "open for business at the usual time this spring and remain open through the season, and is in a position to accommodate many thousands of guests and visitors who will make their pilgrimage to this popular recreational center this summer." Even the American Legion got in on the campaign, its 135 leaders throughout the state being asked to read the news aloud at their meetings.

The efforts worked. Crowds, slow at first, began coming back. In mid-August, less than seven months after the fire, a prominent New York socialite, Mrs. W. B. Walker, told the *Wilmington News* she was surprised. The damage seemed to have been so quickly repaired, she said. Friends had tried to dissuade her from making her annual trip to the Kitty Cottage. The beach had been "wiped out," they said. There was "nothing left." Walker, whose oil tycoon husband had died earlier in the year, went anyway and saw little change—other than improvements. "In many ways the beach is better now than it ever was," she told the paper. "The new cottages are so much more comfortable and cleaner than were some of the old ones."

One year after the fire, the *News* looked back and found "the resort's reconstruction program has surpassed the expectations of the most optimistic." The paper reported,

> Thirty-three residences, ranging in value from several hundred to thousands of dollars, have been built in the area swept by the fire. Many more are expected to be erected this spring. In practically all cases, the new buildings are of better construction and type than those burned.
>
> A total of 3,750 feet of boardwalk have been

rebuilt by the town, through CWA aid. This includes
all streets on which homes have been rebuilt. The
town has also replaced all fire equipment, about
half of the total amount, destroyed in the fire, and
has cleaned up the area. In erasing the marks of
the flames, 15 carloads of debris were removed.

Some changes were obvious to annual visitors. After the
Oceanic Hotel burned, the Tide Water Power Company gave
up on the site and sold it. Subdivisions were built in place of
the majestic structure. Now, the island had only one large
hotel, the Seashore.

An even bigger change, though, was the state's purchase
of the causeway from the mainland to Harbor Island and the
removal of its tolls. The state also announced with great fan-
fare—and no doubt some trepidation—that it would soon
build an automobile bridge to Wrightsville Beach itself.

Tom Wicker well remembers the Wrightsville Beach
of the late 1930s and gives testimony to the island's quick
cleanup. In fact, he doesn't recall the fire, which occurred
when he was just eight.

As a boy, Wicker often got to ride from the small town
of Hamlet to Wrightsville Beach. It was not the closest beach
to Hamlet. But his father worked for the Seaboard Air Line
Railway in the 1930s, which meant the family could ride the
train for free, and the Seaboard connected Hamlet and Wilmington. The little train was called the Boll Weevil.

"It's not a very active line, but a part of it is very straight;
it's famous in the railroading industry for being so straight,"
Wicker remembers now from his home in Vermont. "When
you got to Wilmington, I don't know why this was, but you

transferred to a trolley line and would take the trolley. It ran right down the middle of the beach, with cottages on either side."

The free railroad ride actually was but one of two reasons Wicker was allowed to go to the beach. The other was oversight. "Mrs. Roy Muse, who lived in my hometown with her family, she owned one of those . . . so-called cottages in those days. I'm talking about the '30s. What it was was a big boardinghouse. We probably ate breakfasts there, I'm sure. I remember lunches and dinners and big tables, big community tables. It was very good food, and quite inexpensive."

Either Wicker's mother or Mrs. Muse would take him on the trip to Wrightsville when he was young. Mrs. Muse's son, Roy, was only a few years older than Wicker, and the two were inseparable at the beach. Wicker picked up a skill:

The arrival of automobiles on the island in 1935 was one of the most character-changing events in Wrightsville Beach's history. It would soon mean the end of the old beach trolleys. The last one ran in 1940.
NEW HANOVER PUBLIC LIBRARY, ROBERT M. FALES COLLECTION

"Once, I learned to go crabbing down there. We attached some bait or fish to a string, lowered the string, and then would pull it out with the crab attached. I would take them and give them to Mrs. Muse, and they would probably find their way onto her table."

One moment stands out from his youngest days. "I recall once my father took me swimming down there. I recall that the Wrightsville surf was regarded as a pretty rough, big surf." It wasn't necessarily dangerous, but it was a lot rougher than, say, the surf at Carolina Beach. "So it was not strange that my father would be in there to watch out for me, though he wasn't a good swimmer either." Years after that swim, about a half-century later, he wrote about it. He was by then a columnist with the *New York Times*, and it was clear the event was both his earliest memory of the beach and his most persistent. The day was a Sunday "with a delicious sense of illicit freedom" from church, he wrote, and the sun was so hot he had to wear a shirt with his scratchy woolen trunks. His father's hand gave him a sense of safety and certainty against the high waves. Years later, that memory would persist more than any later teenage carousing at the beach or at Lumina.

He wrote of day trips to the beach: "We could take the Boll Weevil in the morning, switch to the trolley for the ride over the causeway to Wrightsville Beach, swim and play the jukebox and eat hot dogs at the Lumina, then dash for the trolley and the Boll Weevil, for the long trip home." If a family went for a day or two, the trolley would deliver them practically to the steps of an old wooden or shingled boardinghouse cottage. "From its high porch and comfortable rockers, the grown-ups could sit and talk while looking out over the ocean or the sound between island and mainland. At dinnertime, in the middle of an eternal summer day, the table would be laden with fried fish, deviled crab, chicken, vegetables, iced tea, pie and cakes."

Wrightsville was like most of the Carolina islands, little developed and offering bargains. "My family used to drive down to Myrtle Beach," Wicker remembers now. "All of these beaches at that time were very much alike. The four of us— my father, mother, sister, and I—we could drive down there and have a glorious seafood lunch, probably for no more than 50 cents a head."

Wrightsville was terrific. "It was a great place to go, particularly because by the time I got up to being a teenager, I was allowed to go by myself."

The old days were changing at Wrightsville.

Lumina long had provided large orchestras during the beach season but not nationally known ones. Radio broadcasting, which began in 1923, started to make stars of the musicians and also created the Big Band era of the 1930s and 1940s. So by 1935, the year after Wrightsville's big fire, the real Big Band names began coming to Lumina—Paul Whiteman, Guy Lombardo, Jimmy Dorsey, Tommy Dorsey, Sammy Kay, Vincent Lopez, Jan Garber, Hal Kemp, Ted Weems, Stan Kenton, Kay Kyser, Glen Gray, and many others.

Musical styles were changing, and so were bathing suits. In the early days of the 20th century, only men's bathing suits could be rented from Lumina. When women went into the ocean, they usually lifted their skirts slightly and waded into the surf. By the early 1920s, they wore stockings and bloomers with a tunic over the top and often a girdle underneath. A rubber bathing cap and rubber shoes completed the outfit. By the mid-1920s, however, one-piece woolen suits for women came into use. They appeared in increasing numbers by the 1930s. The suits were not uniformly popular. An anonymous reader's letter to the *Wilmington Morning Star* on June 8, 1931, blasted the attire:

> I see in your morning paper, a notice from Spring Valley, N.Y., about women and girls wearing indecent bathing suits, and I will say as a resident of Wrightsville Beach that it would be a good idea for us to also have that rule here as it is disgusting to see girls and women going along the boardwalk with such indecent bathing suits. I have been all over the United States, and have never seen such indecent bathing suits as I see on Wrightsville Beach.
>
> If I had a young daughter, she would not be at Wrightsville Beach.
>
> They call Coney Island "Hell's Playground" but I never saw a woman on the boardwalk without a wrap of some kind over her bathing suit. I was up to the Oceanic hotel last year watching the bathers, and two very fine looking gentlemen said within my hearing, they would never come to Wrightsville Beach to find a wife. It is disgusting to sit on my porch and see the way the females look. I think something should be done to put a stop to it, just for decency's sake. Please say something in your valuable paper in reference to this.

One wonders what the reader would have thought a half-century later when the bikini—and less—made it to Wrightsville. Anne Russell wrote in *Carolina Yacht Club Chronicles*, "When the Thong appeared on the beach in front of the Carolina Yacht Club, one senior male CYC member (who wishes to remain anonymous) began keeping an extra supply of his heart medication in his locker for emergency use."

Retailing was about to make a leap as well. Lester Newell and his wife came to the beach following the fire, first with a small concession stand on Harbor Island that served people going to and from the beach. Then Newell took over the running of Station One, the small stand owned by the Tide Water Power Company at the first trolley stop on the beach. Newell's became a popular stop at the beach, and Lester Newell soon made it bigger.

Competition emerged for Lumina during the 1930s, too. The Seashore Hotel spruced up its appearance and its musical fare, bringing Don Redman and his Connie Inn Orchestra in 1932—both the first black band and the first Big Band to play the island. In 1935, Mrs. J. A. Snyder, owner of the Kitty Cottage, leased the Seashore. She soon staged a contest to rename the island's only large hotel. In 1937, the Seashore—the second Seashore, to be precise—became the Ocean Terrace Hotel.

Meanwhile, a new entertainment pavilion arrived. The Harbor Island Casino, overlooking Banks Channel, opened with fireworks on July 1, 1933. The pavilion included a 108-by-64-foot dance floor. It quickly introduced dance bands and Big Bands to rival those at Lumina.

The Harbor Island Casino would close in 1937, according to Greg Watkins's *Wrightsville Beach: A Pictorial History*. But it drew large crowds, particular on July 6, 1934, when it held a statewide bathing-beauty contest. Music came from Marian Bergeron, the reigning Miss America, and her American Playboy Orchestra.

Those were significant changes all. But the biggest change for Wrightsville Beach can be summed up in one word.

Cars.

Citizens urged the state to buy the Tide Water Power Company's right of way, which it did in 1934 for $65,000. By the spring of 1935, Rupert Benson wrote, "beach authorities

Cars replaced trolleys, the Mira-Mar Pier was built, and Lumina still dominated the Wrightsville Beach skyline. This aerial picture was taken by Hugh Morton for a postcard.
AUTHOR COLLECTION

realized something had to be done to resurrect this island resort." The state built a two-lane wooden bridge over Banks Channel to the outer island, next to the railway trestle on its north side, and paved it for automobiles.

The impact was immediate. A postcard of the era titled "New Banks Channel Bridge" noted on the back that "the bridge makes it possible for motorists to drive directly to Wrightsville Beach, where ample free parking space is available."

It was time to build roads. In 1936, in part through the persistence of the Seashore-owning Mrs. Snyder, the beach island was widened along Banks Channel with sand from dredging the channel. Waynick Boulevard—named for the state highway commissioner, Capus M. Waynick—was laid along the newly expanded western edge. North of Station

One, North Lumina Avenue was built in the roadbed of the northern extension of the trolley line and paved with the help of the Works Progress Administration. Side streets began to be paved.

The demise of the old beach trolley now was imminent. Wilmington was the last city in North Carolina to give up its electric streetcars, doing so in April 1939. Wrightsville's extension lasted a year longer. The last run was made on April 27, 1940. Tuck Savage, the Lumina dance-floor manager and lifeguard, had made the first run 38 years earlier. Now, he made the last as well.

Other changes came. In 1939, the Tide Water Power Company sold Lumina to Charles B. Parmele, who sold shares in it to Mr. P. R. Smith.

Writing of the "old days," Rupert Benson noted, "There is much to be said about Wrightsville Beach and its grandeur. For she was a grand lady." He found a litany of reasons. People meeting at the Kitty Cottage on the ocean, seeing friends they had not seen for a time. The dance floor of Lumina, where "the great and the small" met for an evening, attired in full dress, coat, and tie. The finest orchestras in the country playing on Sunday afternoons while parents listened and children played on the beach. Sunday picnics, trolley rides, carefree weekends. Motion pictures over the water, children's parades, a grand era . . .

"The auto changed all this and what a mess."

Chapter Eleven

THE ISLAND GOES DARK

Despite the Great Depression, or perhaps because of it, Lumina was a mecca during the 1930s. From 1930 through 1933, Jelly Leftwich and his Duke University Orchestra played all summer to large crowds. Lumina still offered high-quality entertainment for little money. For just 40 cents admission, 20 cents for ginger ale, and whatever it cost to smuggle in some illegal whiskey for those inclined, an evening of enchantment could be had. A 60-cent "combination ticket" was available, allowing both a round-trip ride from the city and admission to Lumina, ginger ale not included.

Perhaps no one has described Lumina in the lead-up to World War II more artfully than the late David Brinkley, who grew up in Wilmington and Wrightsville Beach, wrote for the *Morning Star*, and later went on to fame with NBC News and ABC News. His family had a cottage at Wrightsville, and Brinkley even worked at Lumina. The descriptions in his 1995 autobiography, which focused on 1935, the year he turned 15, were especially evocative.

Lumina was not merely the center of summer social life

for Wilmington and the small towns all around, Brinkley wrote:

> For me, at fifteen, it was even more than that—the
> first summer jobs of my life. First, as a soda jerk
> at the fountain just off the dance floor and over-
> looking the ocean where a six-ounce glass of ice,
> a one-ounce squirt of Coca-Cola syrup, plus car-
> bonated water drawn with a flourish from a faucet
> shaped like a chrome-plated swan's neck, produced
> a "fountain Coke," the aqua vitae of the prewar
> South. At intervals other dancers took time out to
> stroll over to my soda fountain to ask for a bottle
> of Canada Dry club soda, or sparkling water, to
> mix with their illegal whiskey concealed in brown
> paper sacks. Mr. Reynolds, the proprietor, care-
> fully explained to me that the carbonated water
> from his soda fountain was identical to the brand-
> name product that came in bottles and sold for
> twenty cents. Therefore, he said, we should collect
> the empty bottles and refill them from the foun-
> tain and sell them for twenty cents at a profit mar-
> gin of 100 percent.
>
> Was this cheating?
>
> "No," he said. "Carbonated water is carbonated
> water. Ours is better than theirs. Theirs is put in
> bottles and hauled down here to the beach on a
> truck. Ours is made fresh right here. And so ours is
> better." With these contortions the moral dilemma
> was resolved in Mr. Reynolds' favor, and I refilled
> Canada Dry bottles from my fountain.

Brinkley later got a promotion and a pay raise to $21
a month. His responsibilities increased as well. He took the

40-cent tickets to admit patrons to the dance floor. Some-times, on black-tie nights, he was told to keep out anyone inappropriately dressed, "particularly those wearing tuxedos and white shoes, which was often, or even worse wearing the gray suede crepe-sole shoes then fashionable among the young and highly endorsed by our fashion bible, *Esquire* mag-azine, thought not for evening."

Brinkley also illuminated Lumina, in a manner of speak-ing, both inside and out:

Another of my summer jobs was occasionally to switch on a mirror-covered ball suspended over the dance floor so that it rotated while I aimed a spot-light at it, changing colored filters and causing the tiny mirrors to throw little spangles of colored light all over the dance floor. Before the discotheque was invented this was a new and exciting idea that made the dancers stop, marvel at this spectacle of what were not yet called production values.

On Lumina's roof, five stories above the beach and the ocean, was a huge sign with six letters about eight feet high spelling out in 126 electric lightbulbs LUMINA. I knew it was 126 because I counted them when I was given the daily job of climbing to the roof carrying a bushel basket of sixty-watt lightbulbs and replacing the ten or twelve that burned out every day, being rather proud that my extremely specialized handiwork could be seen for miles. My older brothers laughed at the sight of me climbing around on the roof with a basket of lightbulbs. Laughable, no doubt, but it did buy me a glen-plaid suit and a blue shirt with a white collar.

Brinkley remembered the magic, and the mischief, of Lumina:

> One Saturday night at Lumina, the grand old dance pavilion at Wrightsville Beach, Kenny Sargent was driving the women crazy. He was up on the bandstand singing one of his standards, "Under a Blanket of Blue," calling up warm, smooth and moist fantasies of making out on the beach sand . . . *"Wrapped in the arms of sweet romance."*
>
> Behind him, Clarence Hutchenrider played clarinet figures of soft, fluid perfection, and Billy Rausch blew the longest, purest tones out of his trombone.
>
> > *A summer night's magic, enthralling me so*
> > *The night would be tragic*
> > *If you weren't here, to share it, my dear . . .*
>
> They, along with the Glen Gray Casa Loma Orchestra, were arrayed across the bandstand in white-tied splendor, already well known to the Lumina crowd from their movies, radio's *Camel Caravan* and their Decca records. They had come to Wrightsville to play a one-night stand, traveling by bus as all the big bands did then, twelve or fourteen players in the bus seats, sleeping, reading, drinking, all their instruments stuffed into the baggage compartment below.
>
> Lumina stood on, or actually in, the Atlantic Ocean, since it was on raised pilings, and at high tide the breakers rolled in, roaring and sizzling over the white beach and sand and on up under the dance floor. The soft-edged pastel beauty of

the oceanfront, the sounds of the surf, the music, Sargent, suave and handsome and, it seemed, singing to each woman alone about making love on the beach. It simply was wonderful. For two or three women swept up in erotic fantasy, it was too much. They groaned and fainted and had to be carried out to the cool salt air in a memorable display of thighs, satin garters and silk stockings. One young woman pushed up to the bandstand and reached up to tug on Kenny Sargent's sleeve and, in my hearing, invited him after the dance to come to her house down the beach where, she said, he could "relax, put your feet up, look out at the ocean under a full moon and I'll give you a drink."

He asked her, "Where are the people you came here with?"

"Forget them. I've sent them all away. It'll be just you and me under a blanket of blue."

Such dreaminess would not last forever. "Wrightsville Beach was all sweet, all beautiful, but its days were dwindling down to a precious few," Brinkley wrote. "The war was raging in Europe now. Musicians were being drafted to play in military bands, and soon these would be remembered as the last nights of peacetime frivolity."

As early as 1931, the Germans were nearby. The *Wilmington Morning Star* of August 27, 1931, noted that "Louis T. Moore, secretary of the Chamber of Commerce, secured a remarkably clear picture of the DO-X [a six-engine flying boat] yesterday when the giant German plane was passing over Wrightsville Beach." Susan Taylor Block, describing the photograph in *Wilmington through the lens of Louis T. Moore*, said beach onlookers simply marveled at a flying machine superior to anything America had.

In early December 1939, the Coast Guard picked up a 45-foot yacht, the *Lekala*, and detained its crew at Wrightsville. The seven crew members, all Germans, insisted they were headed for Miami on a pleasure cruise. They were released a week later by federal authorities. After the war, however, a newspaper editorial said, "We have always considered it unfortunate that the *Lekala* yacht with its crew of Germans which tied up on the inland waterway at Wrightsville in 1940 [*sic*] was not held for further inquiry. Its presence and its character were exposed in a story in the *Post* at the time. Later, however, the FBI did capture one of those men as he landed from a submarine on Long Island."

The same day the *Lekala* was picked up, a fisherman named, appropriately enough, James Bass told newsmen he saw a submarine off Hampstead, a few miles north of Wrightsville. Bass and his two brothers said they first saw a seaplane dive sharply toward the ocean, fly up the coast, then return and fly over the spot again. An hour and a half later, they saw something rise from the same spot. "It looked like the front of the *Perch* when it was here," he said, referring to an American submarine that had visited. "At first I thought it was a sperm whale, because the front of it looked like pictures of them I had seen. But it continued to rise toward the stern until there was about 75 feet of it out of water and then suddenly it went down again. There was only a ripple left, where the porpoises were cutting up something fierce."

By 1941, World War II came to Wrightsville Beach.

The huge influx of troops to southeastern North Carolina led to a need for housing, as did the ramped-up shipbuilding industry in Wilmington, which soon was turning out an average of 11 cargo ships a month. Each branch of the armed forces stationed thousands in the area—the United States Army at Camp Davis and Fort Fisher, the Army Air Forces at Bluethenthal Field, the United States Navy at Fort Caswell, the Marine Corps at Camp Lejeune, and the Coast Guard at Wrightsville Beach. Thanks to Camp Davis, between Wilmington and Jacksonville, the population of tiny Holly Ridge in Onslow County skyrocketed from 28 to 110,000.

The population of New Hanover County, which includes Wilmington and Wrightsville, had been less than 48,000 but now was over 100,000. Many of the new arrivals, particularly officers, came to the beach. Cottages were winterized and expanded, and Wrightsville Beach overnight became a year-round community. The Carolina Temple Apartments, The Glenn, and the Tar Heelia Inn all were beach cottages converted into apartments, according to the World War II Wilmington Home Front Heritage Coalition.

An increasing number of people had begun spending winters at Wrightsville during the Depression. Still, only 242 lived there year-round in 1940. By war's end in 1945, there were more than 1,500. The town benefited from a number of civic improvements during the war years, including a modern water supply; electrical, gas, and telephone service; improved streets; a modern sewerage system; and motorized police and fire departments.

The changes affected all walks of life. During the summer of 1942, Sunday-evening services at the Little Chapel on the Boardwalk, historically thinly attended, were scrapped in favor of morning services. Both military and civilian families were living on the island now. Many were stuck here. Wrightsville had newly paved roads, but few people could go anywhere because of wartime gasoline rationing. Nor could they take the old beach cars. The tracks had been ripped up and sold to the Japanese for scrap iron.

Wrightsville was fully into the war effort. In mid-December

1941, shortly after the United States entered the war, the town government organized its Committee on Civil Protections. W. E. Singletary, Jr., was named air raid warden and placed in charge of volunteer fire and police forces. He immediately scheduled test fire drills. He also set up warning signals. A three-minute blast on whistles in the town was the signal for an air raid. Six short whistle signals meant all clear.

More dramatically, a blackout was in effect.

German U-boats were engaged in full warfare off the coast of North Carolina by 1942. The submarines would lie in wait for ships forced to swing wide around the shallow, treacherous Frying Pan Shoals, which extend off Cape Fear near Wilmington. The U-boats then would close on their prey if American and British ships or planes weren't able to keep them off.

The coast was told to "go dark." Lights on the beach could illuminate American ships from behind, making them easy targets. Homes turned off their lights for the three-sided blackout; only the western sides could have visible lighting. Heavy, dark curtains were hung at the windows of the Hanover Seaside Club and most other facilities.

Thousands of lights at Lumina were doused. Bill Creasy remembers, "It was a popular place up until World War II. It was the blackout that killed Lumina because they couldn't keep any of the lights. And that's what it was—a house of lights." Blackout curtains wouldn't work. "Lumina was too open to do that. They never would be able to get enough curtains."

The blackout was all-inclusive. No one could so much as light a cigarette or wear a bathing suit on the beach at night. "My dad had a 1941 Plymouth, and he had to paint the top of the headlights black," Creasy says. The reduced lights, called "wartime headlights," were the equivalent of parking lights, throwing only a small amount of light on the ground directly in front of an automobile. Police patrols came down hard on any car owner who wasn't using wartime headlights, he says.

Mrs. Margaret "Peggy" Moore Perdew, daughter of Louis T. Moore, volunteered for the Red Cross at Wilmington's airport, Bluethenthal Field, and helped plot airplanes in the basement of the Wrightsville post office, which opened in 1941. In a 2004 interview taped for an oral-history collection at the University of North Carolina Wilmington's William Madison Randall Library, Perdew said,

> Wrightsville Beach was all completely blacked out. . . . I do remember the most exciting night there was when the shipyard lights went out, 'cause we were told the shipyard would continue around the clock, even during these blackouts that we had all of the time. But they said if the shipyard lights ever went out, that meant it was . . . something important happening, like a submarine or . . . we didn't know. But we were down at Wrightsville Beach when we did experience that time when the shipyard blacked out. And I've never ever been told exactly what it was, but everybody thought it was a submarine off the coast, and I assume that must have been what it was.

It could easily have been.

A series of loud explosions was heard off Wrightsville about 10:30 on the night of March 12, 1942, the *Wilmington News* reported the next day. The explosions were followed by fire, seen by people at both Wrightsville and Carolina beaches. "Some of the residents of Wrightsville Beach said the explosions shook their homes. Others were awakened and saw the fire." The fire was estimated to be 10 to 15 miles directly east of Wrightsville. If the explosions "were the results of an attack on a ship and its sinking," the paper said, "this will be confirmed by the Navy department within the near future."

Word came soon enough. The explosions had been 26 miles off Wrightsville, but everything else was as feared. The tanker *John D. Gill* had been torpedoed by a German submarine, the *U-158*. Spilled oil from the wounded *Gill* spread on the surface of the ocean, encircling the tanker. The order was given to abandon ship. A crewman threw a life ring over the side, one fitted with a self-igniting carbide light, which ignited the oil. Within minutes, the entire ship was on fire. A series of explosions followed. The *Gill* sank. In all, 23 men were killed—19 crewmen and four navy gunners.

Just nine days later, on March 21, another tanker, the *Esso Nashville*, was torpedoed and sank—or at least the bow sank. The remaining two-thirds of the tanker stayed afloat. It would be hauled off, retrofitted with a new stern, and put back in use.

Ten days later, in the afternoon on March 31, 1942, the Americans apparently got a sub in the same area. War Department records documented the action with military terseness: "B-25 (Army plane) sighted sub 25 miles off Wrightsville Beach (Wilmington, N.C.) and dropped 4 depth bombs with result of much oil but no debris. Stayed on scene till 1030. At 1745 2 C.G. Boats arrived and dropped 15 D.C.'s."

By the end of June 1942, a citizens' defense corps was set up at Wrightsville Beach. Commander Thomas Hawkins urged volunteers to sign up. Training classes in fire defense and gas defense were immediately organized. The movie *Fighting the Fire Bomb* was shown in the fire-defense class.

Tin-can collection sites were set up. By 1943, Wrightsville had five metal drums where citizens could drop their tin cans: two in front of the archery facility at Lumina, two by

Newell's stand at Station One, and one on the northern extension at Raleigh Street and Lumina Avenue. On Harbor Island was another. Army trucks came around to make collections.

In December 1942, Lieutenant Commander E. A. Coffin announced that the Coast Guard had begun recruiting 500 men to patrol all the beaches between Wilmington and Jacksonville, North Carolina—on horseback.

They would be led by Lieutenant Commander Juan Ceballos, an ex-cavalryman. "We hope our beaches are never invaded," Ceballos said. "But if they are, mounted patrolmen are going to know how to put up a delaying fight which will enable civilians to evacuate the beaches and enable our armed forces to move in." Ceballos said men on horseback were more useful than men in Jeeps. "Horsemen can go places that jeeps can't—through water, up dunes and through soft sand. Horsemen can travel at night without lights. They move much more silently on the sand than jeeps. They're better camouflaged. Neither storms or high tides can stop them."

Many took part. In *Carolina Yacht Club Chronicles*, Anne Russell wrote of club members in the horse patrol and the Coast Guard Auxiliary and of one particular member's role:

> Everett Huggins helped guard the inlets during World War II. . . . The word was out that saboteurs had landed on Long Island and in Florida. At Wrightsville, Auxiliary motorboats would anchor in the inlets to keep boats from going in or out unless showing a "pass." Huggins was sworn into the Coast Guard, wore a uniform, and carried a signal pistol, on orders to shoot and "run like hell" if a problem arose. He helped ferry the horse patrol to Masonboro Island to guard the deserted strand.

On duty around the clock for two days at a stretch, the guardians of the inlet drank whiskey to keep themselves company, even though liquor was difficult to obtain during the war.

By mid-1943, Wrightsvillians must have gotten tired of the blackout, or at least grown unconvinced of its continuing necessity. A late-June check by the town's police chief, auxiliary policemen, air-raid wardens, and officers and others from the town's "combat team" found voluntary enforcement was not doing the trick. "Many bad lighting situations were found in cottages on the ocean front," town clerk Rupert Benson noted.

Benson and Lester Newell, owner of the popular store and also the town's chief air-raid officer, announced that inspections would be made from now on. All buildings were required to be blacked out on the north, east, and south sides. They also could not "reflect, in any way, a light toward the sea or a sky glow," Benson said. Violators would be arrested.

By November 1943, the restrictions were lifted. Benson announced the decision after talking with Colonel William Pritchard, security officer for the North Carolina district. The town would be removing shades from its streetlights, Benson said. Seaside lighting and outdoor display signs need no longer be extinguished, he noted. Lumina and other locations could remove their ocean-side blackout shades.

Lumina was again a hot spot. Since there were hundreds of thousands of uniformed men in the area and thousands of workers at the shipyard, name acts often appeared: Kay Kyser, Vaughn Monroe, Tommy Tucker, Gene Krupa, Jack Teagarden, Ray McKinley, Guy Lombardo and his twin pianos, and many others. Young dancers now were doing the jitterbug.

The Carolina coast seemed safer, but the war was not

over. Reminders were everywhere apparent on Wrightsville, from civilian sacrifices to the heavy military contingent in the area.

Maneuvers over the Wrightsville surf cost one fighter pilot his life on March 7, 1945. Second Lieutenant Sidney V. Alley, piloting an Army Air Forces P-47, died when his wing-tip snagged a wave while he was completing a low, banking turn over the water. The *Morning Star*, quoting witnesses, said the plane shed its wings and part of its motor as it bounced through the surf. The fuselage drove onto the beach, broke in two at the cockpit, and hurled its occupant on the sand.

Soon, though, the war wound down. The effect on Wrightsville was dramatic. Helen W. McCarl, writing in *A History of The Little Chapel on the Boardwalk, 1907–1977*, noted, "When the winter of 1944 and 1945 arrived the [church's] attendance had decreased considerably. . . . With the ending of the war there was a general exodus from the beach so that through the winter of 1946, the morning services were discontinued."

Chapter Twelve

ESCAPING DONORA'S DEADLY SMOG

Donora, Pennsylvania, lies 30 miles south of Pittsburgh and was best known, at least until October 1948, as the home of baseball player Stan Musial. The star of the St. Louis Cardinals had just completed his sixth full season, and possibly his best. He led the National League with a .376 batting average. In fact, he led the league in nine of the 10 most important statistical categories, falling just one homer short of the home-run lead, or it would have been all 10. Musial shortly would be awarded his third Most Valuable Player award. He had put Donora on the map.

But in late October, Donora became national news for a bizarre tragedy. A mysterious smog settled over the thriving mill town of 14,000 on October 26. The smoke-and-fog combination grew so thick it was hard to see the players at the Saturday-afternoon high-school football game a few days later.

Residents developed respiratory problems and with frightening speed began dying. Newspapers reported that 20 people—some said 21—died within a few days. Six thousand more became ill or were hospitalized with severe abdominal cramps, splitting headaches, nausea, and vomiting. Elderly people with respiratory ailments found themselves choking and coughing up blood. Even houseplants and family pets died. The experts were clueless.

In time, the killer smog was traced to emissions from a zinc plant belonging to a U.S. Steel subsidiary, American Steel & Wire Company. The emissions were made deadly by a temperature inversion. The ground was warmer than the air, an ordinary situation, but this one lasted an extraordinarily long time. Since there was virtually no wind in the valley, the poisons remained trapped in a low-lying fog. For more than five days, there was no escape. Not until the early-morning hours of Halloween did the Donora Zinc Works shut down its furnaces—just hours before rains finally dispersed the smog.

The incident would help spur America's first environmental laws. But now, in November 1948, more than a third of the town was sick and in need of fresh air. Few had the means to get it. One who did was the father of baseball player Musial. Jan Finkel, writing in "The Baseball Biography" on *The Society for American Baseball Research* website, explained, "Lukasz Musial . . . at 58 years old had been retired for four years and had already had several strokes. He and [his wife] Mary moved in with Stan and [his wife] Lil in St. Louis to escape the deadly air, but it didn't help. Lukasz had another stroke on December 17, fell into a coma, and died on December 19."

Everyone wanted to escape "the Donora Smog." But how?

Wrightsville Beach entered the picture at a meeting of the Wilmington Junior Chamber of Commerce. L. C. "Yi" LeGwin turned to his buddy, Bill Broadfoot, as the latter remembered during a newspaper interview nearly half a century later, and said, "This may sound cuckoo but what do we have that those people don't have? Lots of air and sunshine."

LeGwin proposed inviting 50 Pennsylvanians to a week at the beach.

For free.

Broadfoot, president of the Jaycees, presented the idea to the group. It was quickly approved. On November 2, 1948, just one week after the Donora Smog appeared and only days after it left, Jaycees secretary John H. Farrell called Donora mayor A. Z. Chambon with the offer. Chambon, grateful, quickly passed on the invitation. On November 7, Elizabeth Ostrander, secretary of the Donora Board of Health, was back with the details: Physicians had chosen the smog victims most in need of help, and 21 so far had said yes, they would come to Wrightsville Beach.

The offer of Southern hospitality became national news. The National Broadcasting Company aired the story. Readers of the *New York Times* opened their November 8 paper to this report:

> DONORA, Pa., Nov. 7 (AP)—Twenty-one residents who became ill in the smothering smog which resulted in nineteen deaths last week in this mill town will soon leave for a week's rest in North Carolina.
>
> An invitation for as many as fifty to spend a week in the South, with all expenses paid, was extended soon after the disaster by the Junior Chamber of Commerce of Wilmington, N.C., and the Chamber of Commerce of Wrightsville Beach, N.C.
>
> Only ten accepted the offer immediately. Others said they either did not want to leave home or were afraid to fly. However, eleven names were

added to the roll over the week-end.

Elizabeth Ostrander, secretary of the Board of Health, said the twenty-one now signed for the trip would leave by plane Wednesday or Thursday.

"I believe there will be a second group of twenty to thirty who will go when the first group returns," Miss Ostrander said. "All are being selected by our doctors so the ones who need the rest most will be benefited. It's truly a wonderful example of Southern hospitality."

In North Carolina, volunteers were stepping up. Restaurateur George Saffo offered a free arrival dinner at Saffo's. Paul Marshburn and his orchestra would add either a dance or concert. Frank Jones of J&L Transportation offered to transport all baggage to and from the beach; Emerson Lewis of E. R. Grocery offered unlimited eggs and cereal; White Ice Cream and Milk Company would give everyone ice cream and milk; Fox's Bakery would provide bakery goods. Johnnie Mercer's Fishing Pier offered free fishing. A giant oyster roast, a free movie, boating trips, and sightseeing tours to Orton Plantation also were lined up.

By November 10, more were on board. O'Crowley's Cleaners offered free laundry and dry cleaning to the visitors. Jimmie's Produce offered free vegetables. There were offers of free haircuts and free soap. Rehder's Florists would bring flowers to women upon arrival. The *Wilmington Morning Star* would provide newspapers, and the Wrightsville Beach Chamber of Commerce, now co-host with the Wilmington Jaycees, would arrange to get the Pennsylvanians copies of their hometown paper as well.

Capital Airlines even offered a free flight from Pittsburgh to Norfolk, Virginia. National Airlines would complete the trip, again for free, from Norfolk to Wilmington.

There was one hitch. On November 10, the Civil Aeronautics Board (CAB), citing a rule against free passes, which had been abused in the past, refused to allow the free flights. The free week's vacation was in danger. Wilmington mayor E. L. White hurriedly telegraphed President Harry Truman at Key West, Florida, on the evening of November 10. His annoyance was evident even through the choppy construction of telegraph writing: "City of Wilmington, Wilmington Junior Chamber of Commerce and resort town of Wrightsville Beach invited 50 victims of recent smog disaster Donora, Pa., to a week of sun and fresh air at Wrightsville all expenses paid. Capital Airlines and National Airlines agreeable to fly smog victims roundtrip to Donora and Wilmington free of charge if we can clear permission through Civil Aeronautics Board, Washington. CAB refused permission today. Wilmingtonians indignant that they are refused opportunity to follow through with their emergency mission. We respectfully appeal to you for assistance in this matter."

Four days later, a solution short of presidential intervention appeared. A November 14 article in the *Sunday Sun* of Baltimore quoted a CAB spokesman as saying the convalescents likely could get around the rule. The *Sun* reported, "All they have to do, he said, is apply for an exemption from the Civil Aeronautics clause which says airlines can't issue passes on their planes. The CAB, he continued, has authority to grant the request and in a case like this, very probably would do so without delay."

By the next day, Monday, November 15, arrangements were set up. The Jaycees could get their flight, though they would have to pay a nominal fee. A chartered Capital Airlines DC-3 could fly 21 smog victims round trip for $1,000. The Jaycees would raise the money from contributions.

But Tuesday, another kink appeared. In Donora, the invitations were still being extended. The number of attendees would not be 21 but closer to the full 50 who had been invited. The DC-3 would be too small. Broadfoot got Capital Airlines to bump it up to a 60-passenger DC-4. That meant the cost would be bumped up, too, to $2,000, which Broadfoot called Capital's "rock-bottom cost."

All was set. Donora was "very, very grateful" to those offering the trip, Elizabeth Ostrander told the *Morning Star*. "They certainly have gone to a lot of trouble and expense for us and everyone really appreciates their efforts. All of the people who are going to make the trip were ill during the smog. We are trying to choose those who suffered most. Physicians have recommended the cases to the board of health so we can be as fair as possible."

Steve Kostelek, described as being about 60 years old, was one. He was bubbling over. "It's wonderful. It's wonderful," he told the paper. "Why, I've never been in an airplane before. Just think of that! And now, by golly, I'm going to North Carolina. It's just wonderful."

At 12:15 P.M. on Thursday, November 18, 1948, a plane full of Pennsylvanians bundled in overcoats took off from Pittsburgh. A reporter from the *Pittsburgh Post-Gazette* and even a newsreel photographer recorded the scene. Several photographers accompanied the group. They arrived at Bluethenthal Field less than three hours later, at 3 P.M. It had been a good flight. Pilot Frank Cox said they had flown nearly all the 500 miles at 8,000 feet.

The arrival was even better. Wilmington and Wrightsville dignitaries were there. So was the Wilmington Junior High School Band.

Forty visitors from Donora disembarked from the Capital Airlines plane, which had "Good WILLmington Mission" emblazoned on its fuselage. Most of the 40 were over 50 years of age. But they ranged from 26-year-old Kaye Weir to 74-year-old Lydia Little. They spread out in front of the plane for photographers. Flowers were held by all the women, including Mrs. Regina Dougert, the tour's director and a nurse of the Donora Health Department. Radio station WGNI, affiliate of the Mutual Broadcasting System, recorded the arrival for possible use on coast-to-coast hookup. There was talk that NBC might broadcast it.

Wilmington mayor pro-tem E. L. James Wade and city manager J. R. Benson led the delegation. Also on hand were Wrightsville Beach mayor Raiford Trask, Jaycee president Broadfoot, Azalea Festival chairman and photographer Hugh Morton, Wilmington Chamber of Commerce president W. G. Broadfoot, Sr., and executive secretary John H. Farrell, and Wrightsville Chamber of Commerce president Mrs. Russell Wood.

One of the youngest visitors, Elizabeth Chiedor, a 27-year-old mother of two described in the *Morning Star* as a "comely blond," was thrilled beyond words. "We never expected any welcome as big as we got. It's wonderful. I'll remember it as long as I live."

The week would get bigger.

The visitors piled into cars for a police-escorted motorcade to dinner at Saffo's. Afterward, they headed to the beach. Groups ranging from three to eight people were put up in heated apartments and homes in the area around Lumina.

In a figurative sense, the red carpet was rolled out, the royal treatment was given, and the key to the city was awarded. Everyone wanted to help the visitors—"the Donorians," as they came to be called in the newspaper.

On Friday, festivities began in earnest. The group visited Orton Plantation, riding out in a motorcade supplied by the Wilmington Jaycees, the Wrightsville Beach Lions Club, and beach residents. The Sprunt family gave the visitors a tour of the gardens, mansion, and graveyard.

11-19-1948 ❦

WILMINGTON, N. C., FRIDAY, NOVEMBER 19, 1948

HAPPY DONORA SMOG GROUP RECORDED BIG RECEPTION

PICTURED ABOVE IS THE group of Donora, Pa., smoke and fog convalescing patients after they had alighted yesterday afternoon at Bluethenthal airport from a special DC-4 Capital Airlines plane. The woman at the far left is Mrs. Regina Dougert, nurse of the Donora city health department, who is in charge of the group. There are 40 victims in the party which will stay at Wrightsville Beach for a week at the expense of the Junior Chamber of Commerce. (Staff Photo).

Rousing Welcome Given 40 Smog Victims As They Arrive For Vacation At Beach

Forty citizens of Donora, Pennsylvania, victims of a mysterious but deadly smog that killed at least 20 people, arrive on a Capitol Airlines DC-4 in 1948. The 40 were recipients of a free week at the beach from Wilmington and Wrightsville groups. "It's wonderful. It's wonderful," one 60-year-old man said. "Why, I've never been in an airplane before. Just think of that! And now, by golly, I'm going to North Carolina. It's just wonderful."

WILMINGTON *MORNING STAR*

Then it was on to dinner at the Trade Winds Restaurant at the beach. It may well have been the first seafood dinner for many of the guests from western Pennsylvania. The next day's *Wilmington Morning Star* ran a picture taken by Hugh Morton at the restaurant. It bore the caption, "DONORIANS STUDY OYSTER OPENING." The caption identified D. J. George as the host and said he and a servant were "opening the oysters with a simple twist of the wrist. Seated, left, and looking on with much interest, are Mr. and Mrs. Charles Maund, and Mr. and Mrs. J. L. Stacy, at the right." In truth, while the Maunds looked interested, Mrs. Stacy seemed to be studying her soup bowl.

After dinner, some guests went to see *Black Arrow* at the Carolina movie theater. It likely was a crowd-pleasing choice. The movie version of the Robert Louis Stevenson novel featured Louis Hayward, George Macready, Janet Blair, and lots of swordplay. Afterward, some guests attended a dance at the Cape Fear Artillery Armory, a benefit for the Wilmington Sea Scouts sponsored by the Wilmington Optimist Club.

Alice Words, 70, was amazed at the reception that day. "I thought I'd just sit by myself on the shore all week and crochet—now look at this!" She added somewhat ruefully, "I wish my old man was along."

On Saturday, Wrightsville mayor Trask took about 15 Donorians for a deep-sea fishing expedition aboard his private yacht, the *Sea Boots*. Everyone got a yacht cruise. All 40 cruised up and down the Intracoastal Waterway and into the Cape Fear River on one of four yachts.

On Sunday, the visitors had their choice of churches at Wrightsville or in Wilmington. Then they got an afternoon bus tour of Wilmington, courtesy of the Queen City Coach Company. Seeing the historic sites of the city must have been impressive. But it may not have been the highlight of the day. The Donorians learned by long-distance calls home that snow flurries were falling in Donora even as they were, in the words of the *Morning Star*, "basking in sunshine along the strand."

On Monday, two Donorians, Sam Heller and Tony Zobich, were guests at an Optimist Club meeting and shared their stories. Heller's was particularly noteworthy. He was one of the first of the Donora residents to be affected by the smog. He told the club he had spent considerable time in an oxygen tent. Many already knew. A picture showing him in a hospital bed had appeared in *Life* magazine shortly after the disaster.

On Monday evening, D. M. George, owner of Trade

Winds, threw another oyster roast for the guests. Newspapers did not report whether or not the Donorians were still studying the oyster openings.

Tuesday brought a tour of Airlie, the famed country estate and gardens on the mainland, by one of the owners, Mrs. William A. Corbett. The *Morning Star*, reporting the next day, gave an indication of how charmed the visitors' week was: "They really got a break in the inclement weather that prevailed throughout yesterday, because when their cars passed through the gate at 'Airlie' and they were met by the caretaker, W. C. Taylor, the rain ceased and did not resume until their cars were passing out through the gate."

Then it was back to the beach. First was an ice-cream soda party at Newell's novelty center at Station One, where host Lester Newell gave the visitors "all they could eat and drink." Then, at 8 P.M., a bingo party was held at the nearby S&S Bingo stand, where the Donorians won prizes donated by 11 local merchants. By now, they must have been exhausted. Before bed, there was still a private showing of a 15-minute motion picture of the bulb-growing industry of New Hanover County. At least it wasn't 30 minutes.

The week at the beach was winding down. Plans were announced for a mammoth farewell party and dance Wednesday evening. The public was encouraged to come down and meet the Donorians about whom they had been reading all week.

Before the farewell came a special meal. The guests had been asking for Southern fried chicken, so the organizers put out requests for chickens. Chickens came flooding in—live chickens, dead chickens, even cooked chickens, more than enough for the Donorians to have their noon dinner at the Nautilus at Wrightsville Beach. Broadfoot remembered years later, "My Lord, I never saw so many chickens in my life. . . . I had to ask them to stop bringing chickens."

The group had a private final dinner on Wednesday, a 6:30 P.M. pig roast at Trade Winds. Harry Hayden, a reporter for the *Morning Star*, was present and got numerous assessments of the week.

Regina Dougert, the registered nurse who accompanied the party, said the patients were much improved physically and psychologically. She pointed to Clifford Devore, 47, who probably had been the most emaciated member of the group when he arrived. Devore proudly said he had put on nine pounds. His companion Samuel Rosenthal, 52, had gained five pounds.

The eldest guest, Lydia Little, told Hayden she never dreamed that people who were absolutely unknown to the Donorians a week ago could have been so hospitable, so generous, and so kind. She was planning to return to Wrightsville Beach for her vacation. Margaret Walks, 43, Alice Words, 70, and Estell Harrison, 59, interjected their own appreciation and said they all felt better for the week of fresh air. Assistant Fire Chief Charles Titus, 64, who had arrived as a hero for saving the lives of more than 40 Donorians during the smog, said words could not express his appreciation. So did the oyster-sampling couples, the Staceys and the Maunds. They all wished they didn't have to go.

The Donorians had one more stop—the big farewell party at the armory.

The motorcade to the farewell was given a police escort by Wrightsville chief W. Riley Wiggs, a Wilmington police escort joining in at the city limits. Hayden described the visitors' entrance in the next day's paper: "With their faces glowing with a healthier look and their eyes gleaming happiness, the Donorians were applauded loudly as they entered the armory last night. . . . The Junior High school band opened the farewell party last night with stirring music as the Donorians entered the armory to the wild applause of the hundreds of citizens."

The four-hour farewell featured dance music by Loop McGowan and his Loop Boys and Jack Pate and his Rhythm-airs. Two drum-and-bugle corps, from the Sudan Temple and the American Legion, also performed. Local radio announcers Lou Essick of WGNI and Bill Guerin of WMFD (identified as F. W. "Pat" Gerkin in one account) were co-emcees. There was also a 30-minute "Ole Time Minstrel Show," which included performers in blackface, still apparently a custom of the time. The evening concluded with a square dance.

The 40 Donorians departed the next morning, Thursday, November 25—appropriately enough, Thanksgiving Day. More than 500 citizens showed up at the airport to see them off.

Nurse Dougert said again that each of the 40 had improved "tremendously" during the week at the beach. "They look better and feel better," she noted. "The people of New Hanover County have our deepest appreciation. They have been wonderful to us."

Stanley Wani, 41, more than agreed: "If I didn't have a wife and three children in Donora, I'd stay down here. I'd even live in one of the vacant beach houses just to be here. The people are wonderful, friendly."

Lydia Little was by now a favorite of the newspaper. The eldest visitor paused on the stairway of the DC-4 and told one of the well-wishers, "I'll never forget this trip. It's been wonderful, more than I can ever say. I hope to come back again."

Two women kissed Wilmington mayor pro-tem E. L. Wade on each cheek, a visual opportunity too good to pass up. The *Morning Star* ran the photograph at the top of the next day's front page, under the caption, "Mayor Pro Tem Says Goodbye."

At 10:06 A.M., the Capital Airlines DC-4 took off and headed north. Wrightsville Beach clerk-treasurer Rupert L. Benson wrote years later of the moment, "The people of Wilmington and Wrightsville Beach opened their hearts, home, pocketbooks and businesses with open arms. . . . As the D.C. 4 lifted to the air and a dip of its wing to a happy farewell, all who had helped felt warm inside as our forty friends of Donora, P.A., said goodbye."

The "Good WILLmington Mission" ended up winning the national Junior Chamber of Commerce's award for the best project of 1948. But it was not about awards or money, Billy Broadfoot told the *Wilmington Star-News* in 1997, some 49 years later. Broadfoot remembered LeGwin's initial suggestion and the enthusiasm that surrounded it. No one questioned paying the $2,000 for the plane, he said: "Price didn't even enter into it." Broadfoot noted that two women from Donora returned to sing at several civic clubs to show appreciation. One man even moved to Wilmington.

The week was still remembered in Donora as well. John Lignelli was the town's mayor in 1997. He had been 26 at the time of the trip, and though he hadn't gone, he remembered the town's excitement. The trip gave mill workers an experience they would never have had. "We come from a middle-class and low-income area. There's very few wealthy people in our area. For someone to reach out and offer to come down there with all expenses paid—they could never have afforded it."

Joe Heller was a 14-year-old Donorian when the deadly smog arrived. He remembered the smog had been so thick his classmates couldn't see the basketball to play in the high-school gym. Even more vividly, he remembered that his father, depressed and hospitalized, had nearly given up his will to live. When doctors came around to give him penicillin, Sam Heller had told them, "You're wasting your money. I'm going to die anyway." But Sam Heller took the trip—he was the man who told his story to the Optimist Club. His son said in 1997 that it may have saved his father's life.

Joe Heller said his family never quite figured out why another town hundreds of miles away would reach out to his community. "There must have been a lot of good, Christian people down there. I don't think nowadays people would have that mentality."

Sam Heller ended up living until 1969, his son said. Until he died, he always made it a point to stop and visit when family vacations took him near the town he called "Good WILLmington."

Chapter Thirteen

HAZEL CRASHES IN

The year 1954 was notable at Wrightsville Beach for the same reason it was notable up and down the North Carolina coast.

Hurricane Hazel.

Even now, the words bring instant recognition, and a chill to old-timers. At Wrightsville, Hazel had a devastating effect, greater even than the Big Storm of 1899, in part because of the buildup of the previous half-century. Packing 125 mile-an-hour winds and 12-foot-high tides, Hazel simply overran the island.

Like other North Carolina barrier islands, Wrightsville has a history inextricably interwoven with hurricanes. That history is measured downed tree by downed tree, flattened cottage by flattened cottage, washed-out road by washed-out road. Periodically, the big, swirling winds that arise out of the tropics sweep up the Atlantic seaboard and bombard the Carolina coast. By the time they go through the absorbing islands to reach the mainland, the high winds, heavy rains, and saturating floods have lessened, perhaps. But the storms will have ripped apart both buildings and trees on the islands, scattering them as if to send a warning to all who might be so bold as to put down roots in the future.

Few accounts exist of hurricanes or other storms on the island before the 1800s. In the two centuries since, Wrightsville Beach has been hit hard by nearly two dozen hurricanes and major storms, according to newspaper accounts of the time and Jay Barnes's definitive work, *North Carolina's Hurricane History*.

One of the earliest was the storm of 1827, said to have blown for 30 hours. Lewis Philip Hall quoted an unspecified report: "The force of the waves was of such strength as to move from their location vast cast iron vats of the salt works that were located on the shore of the Sound. The waves rolled over garden fences twenty feet from the landing."

Worse, perhaps, was the storm of September 1856, which struck just three years after the Carolina Yacht Club put up the island's first structure. It was a "perfect tempest," its high tides coinciding with a full moon, Barnes said. Wrightsville, previously an island of live oaks, no longer was. "The waves uprooted and swept away most of the oaks and left only a few trees standing. Of those that remained, most died within a few days due to the invasion of salt water." The massive storm surge ruined even mainland crops. Waves reportedly reached a half-mile from the sound up onto the mainland at an elevation of 30 feet. The speculation, Barnes noted, is that "this hurricane's floods may have been some of the worst in North Carolina's history."

Until that time, hurricanes had been satisfied with taking down nature's own work on the island. But in 1881, when cottages began to appear at Wrightsville, the storms turned toward man's work as well. A severe hurricane struck the coast on September 9 of that year, passing through the fledgling resort about noon. Here, its winds changed direction from easterly to westerly. The westerly winds were the more destructive, "blowing with redoubled fury, crushing buildings and tearing up the largest trees," according to one account.

Hurricanes of late summer and early fall present the biggest threat, but damaging storms can come at any time. An April 1893 windstorm blew down a cottage on the island, as well as the 100-room annex to the Island Beach Hotel on the Hammocks.

The hurricane of 1899, of course, was Wrightsville's most destructive to that date, overwashing the island and breaking up hotels, cottages, bathhouses, train tracks, and even the train trestle.

But just seven years later, memories were rekindled by a storm eerily similar, with one noteworthy difference. In late October 1899, few people were on the island. In mid-September 1906, many were.

The 1906 hurricane already had caused considerable damage along the South Carolina coast, but Wrightsvillians were largely unaware of what was in store for them. On the morning of September 17, winds were clocked at 50 miles an hour, with gusts to a more damaging 70. Suddenly, high tides were bringing water into and over the streets of Wrightsville. Just as in 1899, the ocean surge swept over the island, into the channel, and onto the mainland. One hotel and several cottages were washed away. Again, the trolley-car trestle gave way. "One unusual account from this storm," Barnes added, "came from Masonboro, where Walter Parsley reported finding large bowling balls in his front yard after the storm. Although the balls were made from a dense wood called *lignum vitae*, they had somehow washed across the sound from Wrightsville."

Bowling balls were not the problem, however. Some 200 men, women, and children were cut off from the mainland for six to eight hours. Imperiled by the raging storm, they could do nothing but wait, hope, and pray. The *New York Times* printed a dispatch from Wilmington that described the terror:

> The storm reached its greatest fury between 6 and 7 o'clock this morning. It came without warning, and hundreds of cottages at the beach received their first intimation of danger upon awakening this morning to find breakers sweeping clear across the beach to the sound and rolling up on the mainland, two miles beyond. A trolley car kept at the beach in case of emergency took about twenty-five early risers across the sound on the trestle by which it is reached, and four other cars responded from the city to a telephone message and brought others across while the waves swept the trestle.
>
> Those left at the beach were afraid to cross the trestle, which gave way immediately after the last car reached the mainland. The storm increased in fury until noon, when the rescue work was begun by a number of volunteers. They sent surfboats across the channel at great risk, bringing first the women and children, and later the men, the last of the number being brought over at 5 o'clock this afternoon.

Among those caught on the island was Sheriff Frank Steadman, who immediately deputized several men. They closed the local bars and began patrolling the island to prevent looting.

But it was nature that did the looting. The *Wilmington Star* reported the 1906 hurricane's damage at "many thousands of dollars," much of it at the south end of the island. The gangways and underpinning of virtually every beach structure were swept away. The mile-and-a-half trestle across Banks Channel and Wrightsville Sound was practically gone. "The storm was the worst in years," the *Star* concluded, "and the tide on the sound side was exceeded only by one foot by the great storm which practically made a clean sweep of the beach the last day of September, 1899, seven years ago."

The hurricanes of 1899 and 1906 were headline grabbers. But the problem was merely one of degree. Every few years, Wrightsville was hit hard.

Wind-driven water from a July 1908 storm, for instance, caused the island to be evacuated and destroyed considerable property. An August 1918 storm brought ferocious breakers to the beach, hurling white spray high into the air and taking out a long section of the Steel Pier at the Seashore Hotel, at a replacement cost of $7,000.

A winter storm in February 1920 battered the island for two days, badly damaging dozens of cottages and taking down six, though avoiding nearby Lumina. "Debris and building material are scattered along the beach from the yacht club to and beyond Lumina," the *Star* reported, "thus making almost an embankment of lumber along the beach in this vicinity." The surf cut into the island in a number of places, taking out support timbers and porches on most buildings. "Those who are familiar with the winds and tides stated last night that never before have they seen such 'cutting' tides." Some homeowners "sold their property there or were negotiating the sale."

A 1932 storm rivaled even those of 1899 and 1906 for dramatics.

Frigid gale-force winds and high, rough water pounded the island for three days in late November 1932. Most of the Ocean Avenue boardwalk collapsed into the sea; the rest was declared unsafe. Old-timers called it the worst storm in years. Estimates placed the wind speed at between 50 and 55 miles and hour, while temperatures dropped to 25 to 28 degrees. This time, the northern end of the island was hardest hit. Homes on the seaward side of Ocean Avenue were cut off from the rest of the island. Not a single home on either side of the avenue escaped the damaging waves, however. Loose pilings and boards were pounded against the underpinnings of the homes, until walkways, porches, and sometimes support piles gave way. Likewise, the pavilion and walkway to the Oceanic were swept away. The train trestle survived this time, though rising tides reached within six feet of it.

Damage was conservatively estimated at $60,000, a figure no doubt flattened by the Great Depression. At storm's end, work crews descended on the island to remove debris and shore up hotels and cottages. The *Wilmington News* of Tuesday afternoon, November 30, noted that the John Hill Cronly Cottage had collapsed during the previous night's tide

Wrightsville Beach has been at the mercy of hurricanes and other large storms on countless occasions. Here two houses are surrounded by water after a 1929 storm.
NEW HANOVER PUBLIC LIBRARY, ROBERT M. FALES COLLECTION

and that other cottage owners had been advised to remove their furniture. It added, "More than 1,000 persons visited the beach yesterday to view the damage done and the activities of the workmen. They found the Oceanic hotel roundhouse and beach walkway gone. Ocean avenue, once a 500-yard-long 'street,' far from the high water mark and several feet about the surface of the strand, had disappeared. In its place was a desolate avenue of wave-washed sand, with porchless cottages perched on long piles on each side."

Wrightsville was spared another major storm for a dozen years. The next one, when it came, was remarkable not only for its magnitude but also for the magnitude of the human response. By now, the island's population was swelled by wartime residents. Moreover, the storm approached in the middle of whatever tourist season there was during the war, on August 1, 1944. Fortunately, news spread that the storm had made landfall at nearby Southport about 8 P.M., so people had time to get off the burgeoning island. Barnes described that night:

> A remarkable evacuation of island residents and vacationers was completed at Wrightsville and Carolina Beaches. It was estimated that ten thousand people were removed from these resorts, and many were taken out in the desperate hours of the storm's arrival. One hundred army trucks were brought in from nearby Camp Davis to assist with the transport as army, Coast Guard, and police officers went door to door calling for residents to leave. Many vacationers attempted to flee in their cars and were trapped in rising waters that stalled their vehicles. The Wrightsville Causeway and Carolina Beach road were flooded, and stalled cars blocked the transport of evacuees. Soldiers

and police worked quickly to push aside the cars and successfully complete the evacuation.

Flooding from the 1944 hurricane was treacherous. Police officers who stayed behind reported that the water measured 18 feet at the Wrightsville Town Hall. Many buildings suffered roof damage. The town's new sewerage project, which was under construction, was covered by sand. The Hanover Seaside Club reported sand four inches deep throughout the ground floor. The two piers were partially destroyed. The state's total damage from the storm exceeded $2 million, and a significant portion was at Wrightsville.

Some damage, however, could not be measured in dollars and cents. Rupert Benson, writing nearly three decades later in *Historical Narrative 1841–1972 of Wrightsville Beach, North Carolina*, explained a painful loss:

One of the interesting pleasures of Wrightsville Beach, when we moved down in 1941 was the board walks. They were everywhere, especially did we enjoy the one at the end of Columbia Street at the ocean. One could walk from the street on to the boardwalk and enjoy a long stroll with the ocean lapping under the walk, the beauty of the gulls here and there. The sunrise or just a relaxing stroll in the moonlight—but the 1944 storm destroyed all of this and the walkway had to be taken down—much to the sorrow of many. The Ocean board walk was not the only one, for there were walkways all over the beach, for it was the only way to get to your cottage, without going through water or sand. On both sides of South Lumina were boardwalks all the way to Lumina. Then on further south, it was such a problem to keep them repaired, with ladies catching their heels in the cracks, stumping your toes over the unevenness, until when the storm destroyed so many, progress moved in and cement walks were built. But, did we miss the Ocean Walk Way!

For nearly another decade, North Carolina was spared. It would prove to be merely the calm before the storms. Seven major storms hit from 1953 to 1955, a concentration so great the state earned the sobriquet "Hurricane Alley." North Carolinians had been acquainted with hurricanes before. They would soon be on a first-name basis.

The year 1953 was the first in which the United States Weather Bureau officially provided names for hurricanes—all women's names back then. The previous year, Wrightsville Beach had been evacuated for the first hurricane of the season, known only as "Hurricane A."

But the second hurricane of the 1953 season had a name, Barbara, and it had top winds estimated at 95 miles an hour. It struck the coast on August 13 between Morehead City and Ocracoke. That was well north of Wrightsville, but winds on the island still were severe enough that Barbara claimed her only death here, that of Huston Jernigan, a 46-year-old department-store owner from Dunn, North Carolina. The Associated Press reported that "fringe winds carried him off a fishing pier at Wrightsville Beach. A Coast Guard boat searched fruitlessly for an hour for his body. Dudley Lewis, skipper of another boat searching for the retailer, was thrown through the windshield of his boat and hospitalized."

It was in this context that Hurricane Hazel arrived during the early morning on Friday, October 15, 1954.

And still people were not prepared for it.

In fairness, it was difficult not to underestimate what was coming. Hazel remains the most severe hurricane to hit

North Carolina. Meteorologists had been watching for more than 10 days, not entirely sure what to make of it. It had devastated Haiti, killing more than 600 people—some estimated the number might be as high as 1,000. Newspapers had run stories about Hazel in Haiti. But the storm had weakened. Then, too, media coverage lacked the immediacy or urgency of today's hurricane warnings. There was no Weather Channel or 24-hour cable news or satellite view for local forecasters. The day before Hazel came ashore, the United States Weather Bureau issued "northeast storm warnings" from Charleston, South Carolina: "Winds will be increasing today and tonight on the Virginia and Carolina coasts as the center approaches." North Carolinians on the whole were not panicked, if they were even aware. Forecasters believed the storm was headed for the Outer Banks.

But in the early-morning hours on October 15, the storm's course changed and its forward speed doubled. Hazel came ashore near the South Carolina line and headed north. It carried sustained winds of 140 miles an hour—at Wrightsville, they would be estimated at 125. As devastating as the wind speed was the timing of the landfall. Hazel came ashore at high tide, and, worse still, it was the highest lunar tide of the year. Overwash would be unlike anything most coastal residents had ever seen.

As Hazel approached, Wrightsville mayor Michael C. Brown called the hurricane tracking center in Miami, as he told the *Star-News* years later. Brown helped an official pinpoint Wrightsville Beach. The official's response to Brown was succinct: "Good God, man, you're dead."

Brown didn't go to bed for 36 hours, issuing an evacuation order for the beach and then trying to get it implemented. The mayor estimated there were 300 people living year-round on the island in 1954, and officials went house to house. Some residents refused to go. "A volunteer fireman

Hurricane Hazel would wash over the island, destroying buildings and flipping boats. As it approached, Mayor Michael C. Brown called the hurricane tracking center in Miami. Brown helped an official pinpoint Wrightsville Beach. The official's response was succinct: 'Good God, man, you're dead.' "

NEW HANOVER PUBLIC LIBRARY, ROBERT M. FALES COLLECTION

and an alderman walked into a house," Brown recalled, "and there were a man and his wife and a 2-month-old baby in there asleep. They didn't want to go. [The alderman] said, 'I'm not going to let this child drown because you all are fools.' " The alderman carried the baby out of the house. The parents followed.

Clyde and Peggy Gentry, newlyweds then and both schoolteachers in Wilmington, had moved into an apartment at Wrightsville just two months earlier. Peggy says now that, while rain fell and winds picked up the night before, nobody was very concerned. "We had the radio on a Raleigh station, and they talked about Wrightsville Beach being underwater—and we had just been walking on the beach," she says.

Police came around to order everyone to leave. The

Gentrys departed about 3 A.M., just shutting the door and leaving. "No one took precautions," Peggy says now. "They thought it was going to be a little storm, blowing on by. No one took any precautions." They drove to Wilmington, parked outside the armory, and listened to the radio for word about school. A few hours later, they heard it was closed. So they headed a day early for an out-of-town weekend trip. Their drive through windblown small towns was eerie, Peggy says. They didn't know what they would find on their return.

What had been a storm was becoming a monster. Anne Russell, in *Carolina Yacht Club Chronicles*, wrote that sometime after 10:30 P.M. on October 14,

> WGNI broadcast that Hazel had destroyed a city in Haiti and killed several hundred people, noting it was much stronger now, with winds up to 130 mph due to strike in only six hours.
>
> At 2 A.M. on October 15 the worst possible situation was at hand. Evacuation of Wrightsville Beach was completed by 3 A.M.; the police left the island at 8 A.M. Water was two feet deep at Newell's, and beach destruction had begun. Communications lines went out at 6:33 A.M. By 11:05 A.M., the barometer reached its low point of 28.68, the water at the Wrightsville Sound drawbridge rose four feet above the bridge pavement, or 14.5 feet above mean low water. The sea covered Wrightsville Beach.

It did indeed. Waynick Boulevard was several feet underwater. The tide swept over much of the island, destroying 89 buildings and severely damaging another 155. The first row of cottages, including many large and elaborate structures, was simply removed. Almost everything between Oceanic and Charlotte streets disappeared. The houses no longer existed. One pier was damaged, and the other was destroyed. The Ocean Terrace Hotel—Wrightsville's one large hotel—was badly damaged. So was the Hanover Inn. Hazel blew out the windows of the Neptune Restaurant, then swept all its furnishings into a pile.

Hazel even blew the LUMINA letters off the roof of the island's main attraction, a symbolic loss.

The town's property damages were estimated at $7 million, including severe destruction to the sewage plant.

Mayor Brown's parents lost their home on the oceanfront. His own, on the second row, was one of the lucky ones. The wind blew sand against the house, where it was further packed by the water, so that the high water later simply swirled around but left the house intact. Inside, though, Brown found two feet of water—and floating sofa cushions.

The Gentrys, when they returned from their out-of-town trip, were stunned. "Over on the causeway, boats were turned over and thrown around everywhere," Peggy says. "You'd have to see it to believe it." Residents weren't allowed to drive on the beach, though they could walk. "It was about three weeks before we could move back onto the beach. There were wires in the street," she says. Like Brown, they still had a home: "We had to dig away three feet of sand to get into our apartment."

That was a common problem, even for the lucky ones. In *One Hundred Golden Summers: A History of the Hanover Seaside Club, 1898–1998*, Ann Hewlett Huttman wrote,

> Damage to the clubhouse was very severe. The entire ground floor washed away, leaving only the supporting pilings visible. The weakened lower supports caused the second floor to sag badly. One of the reasons that the lower part of the club-

house was so devastated was that pilings from the destroyed Luna Fishing Pier acted as battering rams, as they were pushed to and fro in the interior of the clubhouse by the tremendous storm surge. Part of the roof was blown away, letting in rain, which ruined the furniture on the third floor. However, even in this grim condition, the club was fortunate, since many structures fared far worse, including the Carolina Yacht Club which lost most of its facilities.

The problems were far from over. When Hazel left the barrier islands, looters arrived. The National Guard and the state police were brought in. Checkpoints were set up. Some looters went instead by boat or even swam to the island and made off with appliances, cash, and other valuables. Thousands of sightseers traveled to the beaches to witness the destruction, but most were turned away.

Stephen "Jack" Clemmons, a resident of Leland, went sightseeing with friends after the storm. They couldn't get through to most beach areas. "Wrightsville Beach was a big mess," he wrote in the *Star-News* in 2003. "We could not go beyond Babies Hospital. The causeway looked like a marina, with large yachts, sailboats, small boats and pieces of cottages littering the roadway. Downed power lines had snagged many of these, and some of the boats had large holes in the hull."

Brown recalled those post-Hazel days years later in the *Star-News*. Tensions increased, he said. No one was allowed over the drawbridge onto the island for two or three days. A day or two after Hazel hit, a group of residents and homeowners gathered at the bridge, demanding to be let onto the island. The town was still closed, officials insisted. "You couldn't drive. Waynick Boulevard had three feet of sand on it," Brown said. "And we had a curfew. Nobody was allowed to live on the beach because we didn't have any water, sewer [or electricity]." It would be six weeks before all routine services were restored and everyone was allowed back to live on the beach.

One man was insistent on being allowed through to inspect the damage, telling a state trooper, "I came all the way from Charlotte to see it and I'm going to see it." Brown said the trooper responded, "I came all the way from Ashland to stop you. Now go." Brown remembered the exchange fondly. "I've laughed about that many times."

As after the Big Storm of 1899, the Carolina Yacht Club had to be rebuilt. It had no insurance for water or wave damage. Local members sold materials to the club at a reduced price. A new clubhouse, built for $105,000, opened on May 30, 1956.

Others who rebuilt quickly paid a price. The Hanover Seaside Club completed $13,000 worth of repairs—equal to one-tenth the value of the entire building—in time for the 1955 season. Hurricanes Connie and Diane came along that summer and undid much of the work. That was becoming the norm. In 1960, Hurricane Donna did $4,000 worth of damage. Again, the ground floor was left covered in sand.

Hurricane Hazel remains the only Category 4 hurricane—having winds between 131 and 155 miles an hour—to reach as far north as North Carolina, though a number of Category 3 hurricanes have come close to those wind speeds. Hazel's path of destruction was 2,000 miles long as the hurricane swept up into Canada, killing people from Haiti to Toronto and doing $350 million worth of damage. No one died at Wrightsville, but 19 people did across North Carolina, and another 200 were injured. Statewide, the losses were $137 million in property damage (in 1954 dollars). Fifteen thousand homes and other structures were destroyed, and another 39,000 were damaged.

Following Hazel, hurricane preparations and building codes changed in North Carolina. So, too, did attitudes and assumptions. As devastating as they were, hurricanes had to be considered a way of life now. Catastrophic storm destruction was always a possibility on a barrier island.

Not that Hazel stuck around to see what she had done. *Morning Star* reporter Harry Calkins was one of the first allowed on Wrightsville Beach the morning after the hurricane struck. He saw devastated houses, wrecked boats, piers and landings whose timbers were now slanted crazily. He heard the forlorn howling of a dog. Calkins described the surreal scene: "Seen in daylight it was eerie. Cumulus white clouds touched by sunlight stood out against the blue sky all around the horizon. Nature in beautiful innocence denied all part in the catastrophe."

Chapter Fourteen

THE LIGHTS GO OUT AT LUMINA

Times changed rapidly after World War II, at Wrightsville Beach as everywhere else. Most of the military had moved out of year-round housing on the island, but soldiers were returning from war to reenter civilian life. Gasoline was available. People wanted to get out, to spend money.

Jukeboxes, which could play prerecorded music anytime, were pushing aside the Big Band era. At Lumina, though, Big Bands held out until the early 1950s, before television did them in for good. Relmon Robinson, Ennis Robinson, and Walter Hersey had bought the pavilion from Parmele and Smith in February 1944. They brought in big-name bands, though usually for one-night appearances, names like Cab Calloway, Glen Gray, Guy Lombardo, Vaughn Monroe, Charles Spivak, Paul Whiteman, and others.

"After the war," Linda Roth says, "the lights came back on. I lived half a block from Lumina." Roth remembers those years well. Her father and her uncle were two of the new owners. "My memories of Lumina, it was beautiful," she says now, standing in the town's museum, where she is a volunteer.

Her father's family had lived on the beach since 1924,

she says. He was a volunteer fireman. "I would go with Daddy and get in the truck with him to all the fires." She remembers the code for the siren blasts. One blast meant a fire in the north end. Two meant Station One. Three meant the south end. Four, as she recalls, meant Harbor Island.

By the 1950s, the Big Bands were gone, replaced by the likes of Buddy Skipper and the Jetty Jumpers, she says. But Lumina was still the place, even if the LUMINA roof letters did come down with Hurricane Hazel. Roth contests the memory of some that Lumina had to "make do" with state conventions and Miss North Carolina pageants. "If it wasn't still a great place, they wouldn't have come. They would have gone somewhere else."

The changes brought by cars continued on the island.

After World War II, Lumina slowly lost its glamour and, during 1954's Hurricane Hazel, symbolically lost its "L U M I N A" rooftop lettering, as well. Crowds steadily thinned. By the 1960s, though housing a popular bar, much of the building was closed. The large pavilion was torn down in 1973, breaking the hearts of generations of Lumina-goers.

Wrightsville was developing a small downtown near the entrance to the island, including Station One and the blocks to the north.

In 1946, the Crest movie theater opened, the first movies-only theater on the island, though the turn-of-the-century Casino and Lumina had shown them as well. That same year, J. L. Bankhead opened Bankhead's Neptune Restaurant across North Lumina Avenue from the Crest. Roberts Market was on the same side as Bankhead's. But after Hazel hit in 1954, it moved across the street. Lester Newell, who had run the Station One drink stand and sandwich shop, bought the operation about 1943. Then, after a state-run liquor store moved out, he replaced Newell's with a much larger brick building. It evolved into a general store offering groceries, hardware, gifts, toys, and clothing—and free coffee.

In 1953, an elementary school opened on Harbor Island. Churches sprouted up. Wrightsville Beach Methodist Church opened in 1947. Seashore Baptist Church opened in 1955. The Little Chapel on the Boardwalk moved to a larger building on Lumina Avenue in 1951. Inside is a striking three-part mural, *The Miraculous Draft of the Fishes*, painted by Wilmington artist Claude Howell.

Traffic increased. On summer weekends, cars on Causeway Drive crossed the two bridges and came to a logjam at the Station One area. So a branch road was built in 1956. It angled off the main road at the island's entrance, veering northeast and connecting across a new bridge with the existing Salisbury Street at what was now the northern end of the island, by Johnnie Mercer's Fishing Pier.

In 1955, the town's one remaining large hotel was lost. Hurricane Hazel had badly damaged the Ocean Terrace. Now, a year later, Wrightsville's other nemesis struck. A fire burned the Ocean Terrace to the ground. First, the original Seashore Hotel had burned down here. Now, its successor had. For the first time since 1897, the resort town of Wrightsville Beach

The Little Chapel on the Boardwalk moved to a new larger facility in 1951, where it remains today. Though no longer particularly little nor on any boardwalk, the church retains its charming name.

PHOTOGRAPH BY VICKI McALLISTER

was without a significant hotel.

By now, Lumina, too, was falling on hard times. The era of Big Bands and beach trolleys had been kind to it. The era of rock-and-roll and automobiles was not.

Rows of opera chairs were removed from the promenade surrounding the dance floor and replaced with small tables and chairs, according to Lewis Philip Hall. The ground-floor bathhouse area was converted into a concessions and amusements area. The dance floor was no longer waxed and polished every week, nor was the exterior painted every two years. The dance floor reopened as a skating rink.

Even the famous exterior lights—the illumination in Lumina—were removed.

"The old charm was gone," Hall wrote. "The boardwalk

streets, the electric railway, movies-over-the-waves, . . . the sprawling Oceanic Hotel and Station One, and all the other unique features—the very things that had made the island so attractive to thousands of city-weary people—had all disappeared into the past. Parking space, and all the other problems and frustrations of the city had come to this peaceful, sun-drenched island."

In 1962, Jack Lane, J. Lansing Smith, and Mike Vaughan took over Lumina and added the popular Upper Deck, a bar-and-grill with a small dance floor. Much of the large facility was unused. The aquarium was converted to storage.

Meanwhile, former mayor Michael C. Brown, believing a major hotel was an imperative for the resort's resurgence,

The Little Chapel's colorful and striking triptych, or group of three murals, is entitled "The Miraculous Draft of the Fishes." It was painted for the new building in 1952 by acclaimed artist Claude Howell, then teaching art at Wilmington College. Howell refused any payment.

PHOTOGRAPH BY VICKI McALLISTER

The Ocean Terrace Hotel, previously the Seashore, was the island's only large hotel after the Oceanic burned in 1934. Hurricane Hazel badly damaged the Ocean Terrace in 1954 and a fire in 1955 finished the destruction. For the first time since 1897, the resort town of Wrightsville Beach was without a significant hotel.

AUTHOR COLLECTION

began negotiating that year for one on the spot of the old Seashore and Ocean Terrace hotels. The town had bought the land after the Ocean Terrace fire. The idea had been to convert it to a park and playground, but nothing came of it. Brown led three days of negotiations for the Wilmington Chamber of Commerce—some accounts say a citizens' committee—which bought the lot for $40,000. It deeded the property to Lawrence Lewis, Jr., of Richmond, Virginia, head of East Coast Hotels and a former Wilmingtonian. Plans were announced for a $1.5 million, seven-story, 120-room hotel with meeting rooms for 250 people, parking for 160 cars, a tennis court, and a yacht pier. This one, unlike its two vanquished predecessors, would be built of brick.

On March 22, 1964, the new Blockade Runner Motor Hotel opened, named for the fast Confederate supply boats that tried to evade Union forces. The hotel, about a mile from the site of the sunken *Fanny and Jenny*, proved popular. Within a year, a 30-room addition was put on.

In 1965, Wrightsville itself expanded by annexing Harbor Island. In the early 1970s, the town went farther, taking over about 20 acres on Harbor Island from the United States Department of the Interior, converting an experimental desalinization plant into offices, and developing parks and a fire station.

Also in 1965, the Army Corps of Engineers closed Moore's Inlet, already partially shut by Hurricane Hazel. Wrightsville Beach and the deserted Shell Island were merged into a longer island. Developers wasted no time. In

The Blockade Runner Hotel opened in 1964 on the spot of the former Seashore and Ocean Terrace hotels. The luxury 125-room, seven-story hotel and conference center proved so popular, a 30-room addition was added the next year. Seen from the ocean, the hotel resembles one of the fast and elusive side-paddle-wheel steamboats for which it was named.

PHOTOGRAPH BY VICKI McALLISTER

1969, two major hotels opened on the increasingly popular beach. One was the four-story, 147-unit Holiday Inn, built on land made available by the inlet's closing. The other was the seven-story, 160-unit Shell Island Resort, technically a large condominium complex, though its rooms were rented as if it were a hotel. Both would prove popular. Both would also become the center of environmental problems.

The town got a second large retail store, after Newell's, when Mrs. D. D. Redick opened the Redix Better Life Store on the causeway in August 1969. Other changes were afoot. Greg Watkins, in *Wrightsville Beach: A Pictorial History*, noted,

> In the late sixties, seventies, and early eighties, Wrightsville Beach restaurants and bars were in their heyday, mostly in the downtown section but as far south as the Upper Deck at Lumina and as far north as the Palm Room and Sea Dog near Johnny Mercer's Pier. Some of the most popular were the Spot, the Crest's Rec Room, the Olympia, Hugo's, and the Wits End. Restaurants, boutiques, gift shops, and bars made for a variety of opportunities, but the charm of Wrightsville's history wasn't lost on the merchants. There developed a hot dog stand called "The Trolley Stop," a condominium called "Station One," and more recently, an ice cream parlor squeezed into an old trolley car.

While others prospered, massive Lumina suffered. The structure was no longer kept up. In 1972, the building inspector recommended condemnation, saying Lumina constituted a safety and fire hazard. Demolition began on April 7, 1973. Many turned out, saddened by the sight.

Memories flowed. Robert Martin Fales, writing in 1984 in *Wilmington Yesteryear*, remembered being "wild with excitement" when his family disembarked at Station Seven, Lumina's stop, for an annual summer trip:

> Lumina was well named, since it still lights the memory of those who had the good fortune to go there in its heyday.
>
> When we got there, we crowded up to pay twenty cents for a locker and rented bathing suit. Our borrowed suits were identified with a block lettered "LUMINA" printed across the top. As far as we were concerned, no bathing attire could be monogrammed with any more status than that.

Many felt that way, and still do. Years later, UNC-TV public television would produce a 45-minute documentary, *Lumina: Remembering the Light*, with assistance from the Wrightsville Beach Museum of History. The program effectively combined nostalgic pictures with interviews of Lumina attendees through the years. Periodically, newspaper articles are written about Lumina. The theme is always the same. There was never anything quite like it. The loss of Lumina was the loss of a friend.

There is little on the island to remember it by now. Lumina Avenue, of course, which was laid on what were once train tracks, then beach trolley tracks. And the appropriately named *Lumina News*, the town's weekly newspaper. Lumina Station, nearby on the mainland, is a collection of offices, boutiques, and the like. Beyond that, a few small businesses throughout the Wilmington area have taken the name: a dance studio, a construction company, a counseling center, a fitness center, a mortgage company, a realty company, a winery.

The site on which Lumina stood now belongs to condos packed tightly and painted an odd shade of blue with a purplish tint. The only small signs that something may have been here are, literally, small signs. One is the thigh-high commemorative marker for Station Seven, put alongside Lumina Avenue as part of the series for the seven stops. It says, "STATION 7 c.1902–1940. Beach Car Stop for Lumina: Pavilion with Ballroom, Bathhouses, Movie Screen in Ocean."

The other is a state highway historical marker placed a block to the west on Waynick Boulevard in 1992. Likewise, it tries but cannot capture the spirit of Lumina in its two dozen words: "LUMINA. Built in 1905; known as 'Fun Spot of the South'; hosted big bands, other entertainment. Pavilion was demolished, 1973. Stood 100 yards east."

In the late 1980s, Tom Wicker, the little boy who had stayed at the Muse Cottage and played in the surf in the 1930s, returned to Wrightsville Beach. He was a famed *New York Times* associate editor and political columnist by then and had been invited to speak at the University of North Carolina Wilmington. The college put him up in a hotel on the island, what had been the Holiday Inn. Wicker, retired now and living in Vermont, remembers it hanging precariously over the sea. He says it was "dangerous, not to me but to the owners, over time."

More, though, he remembers what wasn't there.

He returned to New York and, in a column entitled "Looking For the Lumina," reported the loss. "Only a café called the Trolley Stop, and here and there a reminiscent high-porched cottage, recalled the Wrightsville fixed in memory, in a time free of fumes and progress and fear of anything save the relentless waves and the occasional jellyfish."

Even the grande dame was gone now. "The Lumina has disappeared with time and tide; I could not even tell where it used to be," Wicker wrote.

He stopped a bearded young man emerging from a grocery store with a packaged sandwich. Did the young man know the site of the Lumina?

"The what?" the man asked.

"I could hardly believe his words," Wicker wrote. They were standing on Lumina Avenue, after all, which must have been named for *something*. Lumina had been the center of activity, home to Big Bands and huge crowds. The young man didn't know of Lumina, nor most likely did he know of the trolleys, "though I had not the heart to ask."

It would not have mattered. Few today know of the trolleys, which stopped running in 1940, or the pavilion, which closed in 1973 and had its heyday nearly a half-century earlier. They were of a different age. Lumina—famed up and down the Atlantic coast, a showplace when the word meant something, elegant at a time when elegance mattered—exists now only in books and yellowing newspaper clips, in albums of old photographs and old postcards, in fading memories.

And in the heart.

Condominiums now occupy the site of the famed Lumina Pavilion. Only a nearby beach trolley marker and a highway historical marker a block away give any indication of the magic once here.

PHOTOGRAPH BY VICKI McALLISTER

Chapter Fifteen

HOLDING BACK THE SEA

The problem with development on barrier islands is easy to explain but difficult to address.

Simply put, barrier islands move.

They break apart, they reform. They migrate. An inlet closes in a big storm, and another one opens. They get submerged here and reappear over there. One end may grow while the other end shrinks. Over years, islands may migrate miles. Sometimes over generations, they reverse course and come back. They also may migrate toward the mainland as the sea takes sand from the beach and overwash during storms deposits it on the backside. It's all a continuous, unending process, driven by storms and currents and winds—and maybe nature's sense of humor.

The Wrightsville Beach Museum of History gives an indication of the effect on this particular island: "Originally Wrightsville Beach consisted of a chain of four barrier islands separated by three inlets, Rich, Barren and Deep. . . . The first recognizable change occurred in the early 1800s, when Rich Inlet closed due to natural erosion and migration. It was located approximately halfway between the northern tip of the island and the present Salisbury Street. . . . During the

1800s a second inlet, Deep Inlet, was located approximately where the Carolina Yacht Club is today, [and] closed in the same manner." The third was moved by man, then closed altogether.

On an unoccupied island, such movement matters little to anyone other than cartographers. But after the addition of buildings—which, generally speaking, *don't* move—problems arise. And if the structures are built near the ocean—which is where people want them—the process is even more problematic. If they are built precariously close, valuable property will wind up in the sea.

Whose problem is it?

And what should be done about it?

If anything.

For the better part of a century now, Wrightsville Beach has faced erosion brought on by development and nature in tandem. In 1923, the first jetties—called "groins"—were built out into the sea. The jetties were designed to trap shifting sands from the north. Five 600-foot jetties were built of heavy creosote-treated timbers bolted together, with huge granite stones at the end. Their placement paralleled the beach trolley line; jetties were built across from Stations Three, Four, Five, Six, and Seven. Later, others were added alongside Stations One and Two. Another half-dozen concrete jetties were built as well, though they proved not as effective because the bolts rusted badly. In 1938, with the aid of the federal government, 16 wooden jetties were constructed, spaced a thousand feet apart.

In August 1927, Mayor George E. Kidder wrote to the *New York Times*, responding to a *Times* article that suggested part of the beach had been destroyed by the migration of an inlet and that building breakwaters had failed to solve the problem. Kidder said no efforts to control the migration of sand had been made until early spring of that year—apparently the mayor was not including the jetties of four years

Wrightsville's first attempt at controlling beach erosion came in 1923 when jetties — called "groins" — were built out into the sea. Five 600-foot jetties were built of heavy creosote-treated timbers to catch the drifting sand. They were bolted together, with huge granite stones at the end.

NEW HANOVER PUBLIC LIBRARY, ROBERT M. FALES COLLECTION

earlier—and that only vacant lots had been lost. He continued, "The town of Wrightsville Beach has recently completed the construction of eleven jetties, five of wood and six of concrete sheet piling, to combat the erosion. Two of these jetties were placed at strategic points adjacent to the inlet referred to. Since their construction several months ago they have been subjected to the stresses of two storms and the recent abnormally high tides prevailing on the Atlantic seaboard. It is apparent that they have not only stopped the migration of the inlet northward, but the present indications are that the inlet is actually beginning to move the other way, reclaiming land that has been under water for several years."

On the whole, the jetties did their job. Lewis Philip Hall, writing in *Land of the Golden River*, said, "For forty-two years these jetties built up the shore line, but due to age, marine worms, and deterioration they became almost useless." In 1965, then, a miles-long sand berm was built over the jetties.

Thomas J. Schoenbaum criticized that decision. Writing in the 1982 book, *Islands, Capes, and Sounds: The North Carolina Coast*, he said,

> Wrightsville Beach is a good example of what a commitment to counteracting the natural shoreward migration of a barrier island means. . . .
>
> The Army Corps of Engineers decided to fight erosion and return the island to its original profile insofar as possible. In 1965 they constructed a 2.7-mile-long berm to create an artificial dune line. Then more than 3 million cubic yards of sand and dredge spoil were pumped onto the beach in front of the berm in a process engineers call "beach nourishment." In 1970 another 1.5 million cubic yards of dredge spoil were added.
>
> The result is an artificial beach of coarse, rough material unpleasant to the touch. Along paths leading to the beach there are signs that warn "Danger Dune Eroded Sharp Drop." The action of the waves reflecting against the artificial berm has created a sharp escarpment. Even this unsatisfactory situation can be maintained only by periodic expenditures of ever-greater sums of public tax money; but the ocean will have its way in the end.

This is only one of many ways man has tried to enlarge the land, or at least to keep it from shrinking. Much of Harbor Island, for instance, was reclaimed from marshland beginning in 1925. The outer island has been extended time and again, the museum notes: the 1936 dredging of Banks Channel allowed Waynick Boulevard to be added; the 1966–67 dredging of Lee's Cut created fill for Pelican Drive and other residential areas; repeated dredging south of U.S. 76 meant additional structures could be built; the filling in of Moore's Inlet opened up Shell Island. All made more beach available for more people. Such efforts, of course, also made more money available for developers.

Some also made problems.

The four-story Holiday Inn was built on top of the filled-in inlet, nearly on the ocean. In time, waters were lapping at its base. Ownership and names changed over the years—it became the Holloway Inn by the Sea, the Sheraton Inn, the Holiday Inn again, and the Holiday Inn SunSpree Resort after renovations in 1995. A 1996 hurricane so damaged it that the hotel was rebuilt and moved back from the sea. This time, the 150-room structure also grew to seven stories high, thanks to a legal fight with the town.

Meanwhile, the $22 million, nine-story, 160-suite Shell Island Resort was built at the northern end of the annexed island. Also meanwhile, the inlet on the other side of Shell Island—Mason Inlet, separating the island from Figure Eight Island—began migrating southward. After Hurricanes Bertha and Fran in 1996, waters neared the concrete resort. Sandbags were brought in temporarily, but waters again neared the foundation following Hurricane Floyd in 1999. Owners asked for a hardened sea wall to be built, illegal under North Carolina law. An editorial in the *News & Observer* in Raleigh said, "Even before Hurricane Fran, many coastal property owners had learned harsh lessons about the futility of trying to stem or redirect the ocean's tide. Shell Island developers were forewarned, as others have been who've built in fragile coastal areas determined to enjoy the pleasures of seaside living. . . . [It] is a lesson to everyone who entertains a notion that the ocean is somehow willing to negotiate on anything besides its own terms."

Finally, as the issue played out in court, a decision was made to move the inlet instead. In 2002, Mason

After Moore's Inlet was filled in, extending Wrightsville Beach by connecting it with Shell Island, a hotel was built on top of the old inlet. Soon, waves were licking at the foundation. The hotel was rebuilt farther from the ocean. Today the hotel is the Holiday Inn SunSpree Resort, shown during a 2007 refurbishing.

PHOTOGRAPH BY VICKI McALLISTER

Inlet was relocated back to the north. The Shell Island Resort was out of immediate danger. Today, a large beach lies to the north of the buildings, with plantings to help stop erosion.

But the most common approach to saving beaches, and thus perhaps the most controversial, is beach nourishment—bringing in sand dredged from a channel or inlet elsewhere.

The State magazine, in a December 1963 article about massive development throughout the state since Hurricane Hazel, noted that oceanfront lots had all been bought up at Wrightsville and that the Blockade Runner was about to open. "But the most important factor is the new beach erosion project, under which the Army Engineers will add from 50 to 75 feet of real estate to every ocean-front lot. This is to be done under a project sponsored by city, county, state and federal governments, and involves pumping millions of yards of sand onto the beach."

Beach nourishment combines issues of nature and economics in an unending debate. One side argues that bringing in new sand unfairly profits island homeowners at the expense of taxpayers in general; it's expensive, it's wasteful, and it causes more problems than it solves. The other side says it saves valuable property, which in turn benefits not only the property owners but local and state governments, local businesses, and the masses of people who want beach property or just a beach vacation.

Jay Barnes, in *North Carolina's Hurricane History*, wrote that beach nourishment represents a controversy over spending tax money that may soon be washed away. "Others, however, believe that beach nourishment can be cost effective and that it is necessary to protect the state's considerable economic investment on the coast. Carolina and Wrightsville

The Shell Island Resort, likewise built in a spot Nature considered her own, found itself endangered as an adjacent inlet began migrating toward it. Owners wanted to build a seawall, and a legal battle ensued. Finally, it was decided to move the inlet back to the north. Today a large beach stands in front of and beside the resort.

PHOTOGRAPH BY VICKI McALLISTER

Beaches are the sites of two of North Carolina's oldest nourishment projects, funded mostly by the U.S. Army Corps of Engineers since the mid-1960s. . . . Though engineers consider Floyd's storm surge to have been a 75-year event, not a single building behind the fortified dunes of those two beaches was lost in the storm."

Two 1996 hurricanes, Bertha and Fran, influenced the approaches to beach control. The storm surges caused beach erosion and structural damage for miles. Barnes wrote of Fran, "A storm surge of close to eleven feet tore down dunes and flooded expensive beach houses. Almost the entire town was underwater at one point. . . . On the northern end of the beach, a six-foot dune was flattened, edging Mason Inlet even closer to the imperiled $22 million Shell Island Resort. Like the other nearby beaches, Wrightsville suffered heavy damages: more than 560 homes damaged, 13 houses destroyed, and 50 businesses damaged."

Nourishment projects were put in high gear. When Hurricane Bonnie struck in 1998, damage at Wrightsville was minimal. "The lack of significant destruction along the oceanfront here was credited to two factors: a moderate storm surge and recently completed sand nourishment projects," Barnes wrote. Hurricane Fran had shown the way. "Costly sand nourishment that became a priority after Fran had fortified much of New Hanover's beaches with new protective dunes and stabilizing grasses." Likewise, during Hurricane Floyd the next year, the Shell Island Resort was imperiled, but no building behind the refortified dune structure was damaged.

The yin and yang of beach nourishment is evident in talking to two of Wrightsville's top managers.

Town Manager Robert F. Simpson says the worst storm in recent years was Hurricane Ophelia, which, though it did not make landfall, spun off the coast for three days in 2005,

A jetty near the southern end of Wrightsville Beach is credited with helping keep the beach from eroding.

PHOTOGRAPH BY VICKI McALLISTER

battering the island. "It eroded and eroded," he says. "We almost had a breach of the dune system."

Simpson says the town actually has very little control over the beach, which belongs to the federal government. The town merely runs it. The beach nourishment program, conducted about every four years, is largely paid for by the federal government. But with budget cutbacks, that is in jeopardy.

"I'm not convinced of the value of [beach nourishment], but other people advocate it," Simpson says.

One recent winter storm wiped out a quarter of the just-completed project, he says. Left behind were long es-carpments—cliffs, essentially—where sand had been ripped out of the beach and carried away to sea. The escarpments, on the center and north sections of the beach, were three or four feet deep. The dropoff was so steep, in fact, that the town had to bulldoze sand ramps to allow people to get from one level of the beach to the other. The escarpments, Simpson notes, went up almost exactly to the point where the renourishment had started.

Simpson recognizes the continual tug of war with nature. The island's migration is part of the natural process, he says. Much of the land has been reclaimed from marshland. "Where you're sitting right now," he says to a visitor in his office on Harbor Island, "is man-made." Town buildings, including the main one, which was an administration office for the desalinization project, are in need of repair and enlargement. The fire station must be replaced. But restrictions on filling marshland make these issues even more problematic than they would be elsewhere.

Meanwhile, Planning Director Tony Wilson has a slightly different take on beach nourishment. "I think we need it," he says. "I know dredging keeps open the channel."

Wilson says there have been erosion issues at the north end, at the Shell Island Resort. Likewise, he says that at the Holiday Inn, "we do see some overwash every time there's a hurricane." However, he says, "our south end of the beach seems to be doing well," most likely because of the jetties.

"As I become older, I become more environmentally friendly," Wilson adds. He thinks more can be done in the way of planting vegetation like sea oats and beach grass and putting up sand fences. Some has been done. Moreover, some streets now allow runoff to go through the surface directly into the soil, rather than contaminate the coastal water. Homeowners are required to retain storm water, the rain from gutters going directly into the ground. The big issues for the town are water quality, storm runoff, and erosion, Wilson says. Beach access is another.

Wilson, who used to live on the beach at Surf City on Topsail Island, knows why people come to Wrightsville. "The ocean is the draw. I don't know of anything else," he says.

Thus, the debate continues. Everyone wants the beach, though they may intend different uses for it.

A number of critics of beach development generally and of nourishment programs specifically use arguments similar to Schoenbaum's. Duke University geology professor Orrin Pilkey, among the foremost, has often reserved harsh criticism for Wrightsville Beach's efforts. Pilkey, writing in the *Star-News* in March 2007, said, "All along our coast the building boom continues, as more and more mom-and-pop cottages are replaced by multimillion-dollar mini-mansions that serve as huge rental cash cows for a few individuals who are secure in the belief that the state will continue to pour mon-

The middle of Wrightsville Beach is subject to huge erosion "escarpments". The three-or-four-foot drop-offs are caused by storms that remove much of the sand brought to the beach for "beach nourishment" programs. Here temporary sand "ramps" have been made to allow people to get from one level of the beach to the other.

PHOTOGRAPH BY VICKI McALLISTER

ey into 'beach nourishment.' As the need to hold shorelines in place has increased, beach nourishment has become more frequent. But nourishment is more than just a costly burden to taxpayers. It is also damaging to our beaches." Nourishment has covered beaches with mud, asphalt, and trash, he noted, and sand for it has been taken from tidal deltas even while contributing to long-term erosion.

Harry Simmons, mayor of Caswell Beach and president of the American Shore and Beach Preservation Association, gave the other side when he issued a statement in 2007 arguing against federal cutbacks for beach nourishment:

> Replenishing beaches by adding sand to the system protects coastal habitat by replacing the sand that marine life needs to live. Without sand on a beach, sea turtles, birds, plants and other forms of marine wildlife won't have an ecological infrastructure in place.
>
> Without sand on a beach, coastal erosion also puts coastal communities and the surrounding infrastructure at risk of devastating losses. . . . Beach replenishment projects are far more cost-effective than dealing with the human suffering and property damage from storms.
>
> But with beach replenishment projects economic benefits also follow. . . . Studies have shown that every dollar spent to repair and maintain a beach produces at least four dollars in taxpayer benefits.

Don't expect the debate to stop.
Nature won't.

Chapter Sixteen

WRIGHTSVILLE TODAY

Wrightsville Beach's "downtown" today is two or three blocks that would have been at home two or three generations ago.

Perhaps no place is more symbolic of that than the island's little time machine of a grocery store, Roberts Market, which has gone by several names. Out front is an old neon sign proclaiming, "Roberts Grocery." On the side of the building is painted, "Roberts Market—Historical Landmark—Established 1919." Some call it "Roberts Store." Many just call it "Roberts."

Whatever it is called, walk in today and Roberts seems not very different from when it was started by a Lebanese immigrant from New York all those years ago. Charles S. Robier moved down south on the advice of doctors who said it would help his respiratory condition. So why is his store called Roberts? Locals had difficulty pronouncing Robier. He obligingly changed his name.

The little grocery has been co-owned since 2006 by Jerry Allen, who has also owned the next-door sports bar since 1994. Allen's full name is Jerry Allen Lachman, but he says no one knows him by that. He and his partner, Allan Middleton,

Charles S. Robier's grocery store, named Roberts because the locals couldn't pronounce his name, opened in 1919. The neon sign out front says "Roberts Grocery," while the mural painted on the side of the building says "Roberts Market." Most people know it as "Roberts."

PHOTOGRAPH BY VICKI McALLISTER

haven't forgotten the store's roots. They have made only the slightest of changes—giving the place a scrubbing and, most notably, bringing in large period photographs, each either three feet long or three feet tall. One, for instance, shows a lady in the surf in the bathing suit of a bygone era. At the front of the store, another shows a beach car full of dressed-up beachgoers. The trolley is rumbling across the trestle, almost toward the viewer. Straight out of the past.

Why change anything else? "It's very old-fashioned, very loyal to customers," Allen says of the store, standing outside his office at the front. "We're home of the 'world-famous chicken salad.' I'm sure you know that." Well, of course. Who doesn't? "Roberts Famous Chicken Salad" T-shirts are even for sale here. It's a secret recipe,

Roberts has moved across North Lumina Avenue from its original spot but retained its old-fashioned charm. It's also kept secret the recipe of its famous chicken salad.

PHOTOGRAPH BY VICKI McALLISTER

handed down owner to owner and kept in the store safe. But the ingredients are right there on the shirt: "Chicken + Mayonnaise + Celery + A Little Magic."

A woman comes in and buys groceries this day, including chicken salad in a plastic container. She goes across the street. She gets in her parked car, pulls out a fork, and begins eating it. Right there. Jerry Allen smiles. That happens all the time, he says. All the time.

Roberts is part of a short stretch of shops on North Lumina Avenue that link the old Wrightsville with the new, trolley days with parking-meter days, the modest beach with high-dollar, high-rise resorts. Jerry Allen's Sports Bar and Grill, next to Roberts, is the old Crest movie theater.

In the same neighborhood are the 22 North Restaurant and Bar, the locally famed Sweetwater Surf Shop, Vito's Pizza, the Tower 7 Coffee Shop, the Baja Mexican Grill, a small ice-cream stand, and the Wrightsville Beach Supply Company. Lagerheads Tavern cleverly works two island favorites into its name—beer and sea turtles—and has a popular sidewalk area. Here, too, is another favorite—the long-established King Neptune Restaurant. According to one source, it began as Bankhead's Neptune Restaurant in 1946, the same year the Crest opened. The restaurant claims it has been "an island tradition since 1941." Either way, it is one of the island's oldest continuing commercial enterprises, along with Roberts and Johnnie Mercer's Fishing Pier, and one of

The King Neptune Restaurant, originally Bankhead's Neptune Restaurant, has been a Wrightsville favorite since the 1940s.
PHOTOGRAPH BY VICKI McALLISTER

its most popular. It was renamed King Neptune in 1961 by a subsequent owner.

Though Roberts and the Neptune remain, Wrightsville is changing, in ways subtle and not.

"It's got a unique nature," Town Manager Robert Simpson says, sitting in his office inside the town's facilities on Harbor Island. A retired air force colonel, Simpson has been town manager since 2005, he and his wife having moved down from Maine to be nearer their grown children. What does he mean by unique? "If you looked at all the communities on the East Coast, probably only eight or 10 are equivalent in makeup and nature," he says.

Consider the numbers, Simpson says. The town has just 2,600 year-round residents. Yet the total value of the island following the 2007 reassessments is a whopping $3.3 billion. The year-round population is actually decreasing as elderly residents die or leave. "Their kids take the money and run. Developers get the property," Simpson says. Developers knock down the old period homes and "build out to the legal maximum." Those expensive homes or duplexes often become rental properties, sitting vacant for more than half the year.

But Wrightsville Beach is hardly a small town. Back in 1980, when the year-round population was 2,781, a busy summer day would bring 12,500 people to the island. Now, 30,000 actually live on the island in summer, Simpson says, and well over 100,000 are here on a sunny weekend day. That's the population of a city.

As a result, Wrightsville has the services one might associate with a town of 10,000. "We have a very robust police department," Simpson adds. It includes 22 full-time employees plus a number of part-timers, especially in summer. Police hardly take the winter off, though, as they are constantly busy with issues of drugs, alcohol, and speeding.

It takes work to keep a paradise a paradise these days.

Near the downtown area, south of Lumina Avenue's intersection with Causeway Drive, is Newell's—or what used to be Newell's, having been replaced by Wings. This was the area of Station One on the trolley line.

To the right of Wings, across Waynick Boulevard, is Wynn Plaza, a beautiful small park and dock named in tragedy. In December 1981, fire, one of Wrightsville's old nemeses, broke out in the three-story Doak Apartments. The fire, later declared suspicious, quickly spread next door to the Hanover Seaside Club. The 75-year-old clubhouse—the town's oldest building following Lumina's demise—burned to the ground. Two firemen were trapped inside. One, Robert M. Wynn, died. Wynn, 28, was a volunteer fireman and an assistant manager of the Blockade Runner Motor Hotel. He remains the only firefighter to die in a Wrightsville Beach blaze. The plaza is dedicated to him and to all firefighters who give their

Newell's Shopping Center, a favorite island store for nearly half a century, was the first thing visitors encountered upon driving their cars onto the outer island, as shown in this postcard photograph. The spot is now ...
AUTHOR COLLECTION

lives. The clubhouse was rebuilt two years after the fire.

On the other side of and behind Wings are an ice-cream shop and the Trolley Stop Hot Dog Stand. The small Trolley Stop, with no tables or chairs, opened in 1976. It is now owned by Rick Coombs as part of a chain of Trolley Stops throughout the Wilmington area.

This afternoon, Deryck Smith is behind the counter. She's been working here seven years. Summers are always busy, she says. The Trolley Stop sells between 1,000 and 1,500 hot dogs a day. "We normally have a line down the street. We close at five, and we're working nonstop till then. We don't even have time for a break." The line moves quickly, though. The Trolley Stop offers various hot-dog creations, all with homemade toppings, and people know what they want. The favorite is the North Carolina Dog, which includes coleslaw, mustard, and chili.

In front of the Trolley Stop is one of the seven mosaic-topped

... A Wings T-shirt and beach goods shop. Though taller, Wings has essentially kept the original appearance.

PHOTOGRAPH BY VICKI McALLISTER

markers that were put up to mark the old trolley line. This one says, "Station 1, c. 1902–1940. Beach Car Stop for Oceanic Hotel, Newell's and Pop Gray's Soda."

The surroundings are different these days. Newell's is Wings, of course. The Oceanic burned in 1934. And the only Station One around here is an eight-story condominium project built in 1976. The 1970s and 1980s brought many high-rise condominiums to Wrightsville Beach, including the Islander and Sea Path Towers. The three major hotels or condominium resorts built in the 1960s are all tall structures as well—the Blockade Runner, the Holiday Inn SunSpree Resort, and the Shell Island Resort. Much smaller motels include the Harbor Inn, the Ocean View, One South Lumina, the Sandpeddler, the Silver Gull, Surf Suites, and others. But the high-rises are an obvious part of Wrightsville's skyline now.

The markers for the old trolley stops are spread every few blocks. Some are tucked behind bushes, and a favorite game of tourists is to find them all. They will never succeed. The marker for Station Four, by the Carolina Yacht Club, no longer exists. Locals say it was hit by a car and damaged so badly it had to be removed.

Down by the old Lumina stop, Station Seven, is another tip of the hat to the island's history, stuck among the condos and duplexes. The Oceanic Restaurant's commanding spot helps make it one of the island's showplaces. The restaurant takes its name from the late hotel. The Oceanic has period photographs on the wall as well. But the more compelling view is out the window. Diners look out over the storm-battered Crystal Pier, the jetties near the southern end of the island, and, of course, the sea, surf, and sand. The Oceanic may be one of the headliners, but other popular restaurants include the Causeway Café, a no-frills spot that is always full, along with Buddy's Crab House and Oyster

The Oceanic Restaurant shares the name of the island's famous former hotel, but not the location. The restaurant with the spectacular ocean view sits next to Lumina's old site, backing up to an old fishing pier.

PHOTOGRAPH BY VICKI McALLISTER

Grill, the Bridge Tender, and the Bluewater Grill. In summer, there's not a spot on the island that isn't popular.

If you look down the six aisles at Roberts Market, you'll get the feeling Charles Robier could still be walking them, stocking the shelves. The grocery is in its second location on North Lumina Avenue, and now it has spent more of its life at this spot than the original. But walking in the door is still a step backward in time. This could be 1919, possibly, or certainly the 1950s. Narrow aisles, old shelving, free and easy conversation with the cashier.

Roberts is packed in the summer. People come in for all the usual fare available anywhere, plus some specialties. The chicken salad, of course. Deli meats, fried chicken, macaroni and cheese. Prime meats are a big draw, from the butcher on the premises. Only 8 percent of all beef is prime, Allan Middleton says. You can't find it many places.

If a customer knows someone at Roberts, he or she doesn't have to pull out a wallet. "We have house accounts," Jerry Allen says, smiling, as if he knows how crazy that is in the 21st century. But here, he can do it. "We're old school. We have house accounts for people we don't see till summer." But then Roberts has always done that. It will bill customers at the end of the month. Some of the accounts go back 50 years. They're on the third generation.

That's the secret and the charm of Roberts. "It's always been very local," Allen says. "Family owned and operated. Homemade food."

The land on which Roberts and just about everything

The Oceanic Pier, battered by storms, is closed to fishermen but restaurant diners can sit on the part over the beach. In summer and on any warm day, the seats are at a premium.
PHOTOGRAPH BY
VICKI McALLISTER

Banks Channel and its boat docks lie behind these cottages and Waynick Boulevard. In the foreground is South Lumina Avenue.

PHOTOGRAPH BY VICKI McALLISTER

else in Wrightsville sits is now hugely valuable. More profit could be made by selling it to developers than continuing to peddle chicken salad and fried chicken. But that won't happen here, Middleton says. Little mom-and-pop stores are about gone, he says. This one's not going anywhere.

Is that a promise?

"As long as Jerry and I are here," Middleton says, "it's always going to be here. . . . It may get a facelift. But it'll always be here because people want it—as long as they want it."

Chapter Seventeen

FISHING PIERS AND THE WATERS BEYOND

On an early morning, long before the parking meters at the end of Salisbury Street require feeding, two lighted signs command the skies. The large white one by the parking lot says, "Johnnie Mercers Fishing Pier," plural, as if it is a pier of multiple Mercers. The blue sign on the pier house has correctly made it possessive: "Johnnie Mercer's Fishing Pier."

That's not the biggest misconception about this pier. Ask almost anyone in town and you'll be told the iconic fishing pier is named for the famed composer of the '30s, '40s, and '50s, Johnny Mercer, creator of "Moon River" and so many other songs. The myth is wider than a mile.

The Johnnie Mercer of this pier was a Wilmington businessman. Mercer wanted to build a pier in 1935, according to Rupert Benson, but was turned down by the town. His widow, Wanda Mercer, said years afterward that Mercer actually ended up buying the Atlantic View Pier in the early 1940s, a few years after it was built. She said that over time, locals began referring to it as "Johnnie Mercer's." The couple had to rebuild the pier after Hurricane Hazel in 1954. They went

Johnnie Mercer's Pier, shown shortly after sunrise, is the island's most iconic image. It is also the most photographed. Just check the postcards in any shop.
PHOTOGRAPH BY VICKI McALLISTER

ahead and began calling it Mercer's. Mercer died in a car crash in 1964, and his widow sold the pier to Bob Johnson in 1996. Johnson has owned it since.

James Neal is at the counter inside Mercer's this morning, as he has been many mornings since September 2002.

The way Neal explains it, Mercer built here, but hurricanes kept unbuilding. "A freak wave took out 610 feet in about 1989 and left it short," he says matter-of-factly. "Fran and Bertha in '96 took out another 200 feet." There wasn't much of a pier left. The town, Neal says, ordered that it either be rebuilt or torn down entirely.

Robert Johnson's new pier opened April 1, 2002, bigger, wider, and stronger. Virtually stormproof. Now, the pier would have a fair fight in a hurricane. "This is the only concrete pier I know of on the East Coast," Neal says of the

750-foot, steel-reinforced structure. "I consider it the crown jewel of fishing piers on the East Coast." No swaying, he says. None. "You will be spoiled."

There is a romance to piers, even among those who don't fish. They offer an escape from worries, a trip out into the beauty of the waters beyond the shore, a place where time isn't kept. The sea swirls safely beneath. Spray caresses the momentary pier walker or the day-long fisherman. Crashing waves drown out all other sounds.

Piers have stood at three locations on Wrightsville Beach over the past century. They have become part of the island's lore.

The first was the Seashore Hotel's Steel Pier a century

The pier house for Johnnie Mercer's Pier includes an old-time lunch counter, busy game room, and gift shop that sells T-shirts, suntan lotion, beach toys, chairs, and even bathing suits. And of course, fishing needs.
PHOTOGRAPH BY VICKI McALLISTER

ago, intended mostly for strolling hotel guests wanting to venture out over the waves. The Steel Pier stood from 1910 until it was lost in a storm 10 years later.

It was nearly two decades before Wrightsville Beach had another. Then it got two, both intended as fishing piers. In quick succession in the late 1930s, the Mira-Mar Pier and the Atlantic View Pier went up.

In 1938, Floyd Cox, Sr., opened the Mira-Mar Pier and Restaurant just south of Lumina, where the Sea View Inn had been. The Mira-Mar, a thousand feet long and built of the best cypress timbers, reached out to cover the *Fanny and Jenny* blockade runner. Mira-Mar was only the first of its several names. Later, it became the Luna Pier—"a name just different enough so as not to infringe on Lumina's trademark name," wrote Ann Hewlett Huttman in *One Hundred Golden Summers*. Later still, the Luna was renamed the Crystal Pier. Wilmington restaurateur Mike Zezefellis bought the property in 1962, renamed the pier for one of his old restaurants, and converted the dining room into apartments. The Crystal Pier came under the control of the Oceanic upon that restaurant's construction. Storms have damaged the pier, so it is no longer used for fishing. But it remains in use. The portion over the beach, still safe, is used for dining. Tables fill up quickly.

Meanwhile, the rebuilt Johnnie Mercer's has thrived. The pier is one of Wrightsville Beach's most famous images. It is a postcard favorite.

Mercer's is open 24 hours a day during fishing season. It brings in more king mackerel and even barracuda than other local piers combined, James Neal says. "I don't know why. Maybe the concrete resembles a reef." Neal recites a long list of the fish in these waters: black drum, red drum, Virginia mullet or whiting, pompano, flounder, spot, croaker, sheepshead, trout, cobia, tarpon . . .

As Neal talks, a steady stream of people comes by wanting tickets for the pier. It's eight dollars to fish. Or a dollar just to walk—50 cents for children.

A man who has rented a rod for eight dollars and bought a ticket for another eight asks about bait, eyeing his wallet.

"I have bloodworm alternatives. That works good," Neal says. He's talking about a man-made equivalent of bloodworms that many fisherman say are even better as bait.

"That's $11," the man responds. "How much is shrimp?"

"Four-fifty."

"I'll take shrimp."

Neal talks passionately about environmental issues on the beach, the knocking down of Lumina, and the end of free parking and fishing from bridges. He laments the slow disappearance of other fishing piers in North Carolina—the victims of storms, increased resort property prices, and changing lifestyles. He says piers need to be operated like businesses, offering specials certain times of year, sponsoring contests, selling different types of bait. In short, they need to make themselves much larger attractions.

Johnnie Mercer's is a small-scale entertainment empori-

James Neal has been behind the desk at Johnnie Mercer's since 2002. "I consider it the crown jewel of fishing piers on the East Coast." No swaying, he says of the concrete pier. None. "You will be spoiled."
PHOTOGRAPH BY
VICKI McALLISTER

um. It has an old-time lunch counter and a busy game room, where several children are already at play this morning. Hot dogs, hamburgers, chicken, pizza, sandwiches, and soups are on the menu. A gift shop sells T-shirts and suntan lotion, beach toys and chairs, even bathing suits. Johnnie Mercer's presents itself as a spot for the family. Parents bring their children, who may play in the game room and eventually learn to fish, Neal says.

Neal himself has been coming for nearly 50 years. "I was nine years old when I came to Mercer's first and fished for big game." Growing up, he had season passes at both Johnnie Mercer's and the Crystal Pier. He remembers fishing 360 days a year at the Crystal. "I would love to see the Oceanic brought back. If I get rich, that will be my pier. That's a better location—closer to Masonboro Inlet."

The traffic is steady this morning. Men, women, and children. Most are here for fishing, a few to walk the pier, and some to sit at the lunch counter or hang around the game room.

As he talks, Neal takes one man's money for fishing, folds over a ticket, marks it, and staples it to the man's shirtsleeve. The man asks, "Bloodworms?"

"I've got bloodworm alternatives," Neal says. "They work. I've caught tons of spot and trout."

"For $11?"

"Yeah."

"I'll take shrimp."

Rick Britt, fisherman *extraordinaire*, is out on the pier. He comes with Neal's recommendation: "Rick Britt is, in my opinion, other than me, the premier 'hook' on this pier."

Britt laughs when he hears it. He does all right, he says.

He's been fishing here 38 years, since he was a child. "I remember, for Christmas, all I would want was a season pass." They were $50 or $75, he says. Now, they're $500. He's still here all the time. "This is the only way. I'm out here every day from March to January." The exception was when Karen was sick, he says poignantly. His wife of 25 years died in 2004.

Easily a hundred or more are on the pier already this morning. Some fish by themselves, isolated figures at work, saying little. Others are in pairs or small groups. They talk, laugh, help with one another's lines.

Britt thinks the concrete pilings really do pull in more fish. He fishes mostly for king mackerel and cobia, and tarpon in midsummer. When November comes, he moves closer in on the pier and starts fishing for drum. He does well. "The king mackerel, I'll clean it and give it away," he says. "Every once in a while, I see an older couple, and I just put a 25-pound king mackerel in their bucket."

Some days are better than others, and it doesn't necessarily have anything to do with the catch. "I like fishing the weekends because my friends are out here," he says.

Britt has the soul of a fisherman. He talks easily but doesn't waste words. Ask him what the best time to fish is, and he'll answer a different question.

"My favorite time is sunset," he says. "I live for sunsets out here. Just peaceful. Beautiful."

Sun- and wind-burned Rick Britt has been fishing since he was a child. "I remember for Christmas, all I would want was a season pass."
PHOTOGRAPH BY
VICKI McALLISTER

Chapter Eighteen

GUARDING THE COAST

Senior Chief John Sesta emerges onto the dock behind the United States Coast Guard station at Wrightsville Beach on a warm, sunny fall day. He has gotten off a 47-foot Coast Guard surf boat, one of the vessels returning from training exercises in the Atlantic Ocean this morning. The men tie up the boats, hose them down, and prepare them for the next voyage.

Sesta oversees 30 enlisted men and 20 reservists at Wrightsville Beach. The station is responsible for a 45-mile stretch of shoreline from the middle of Topsail Island to the north to the Cape Fear River at the south—or even farther if need be—as well as 50 miles out into the ocean. That's well over 2,000 square miles of responsibility. And throw in the Intracoastal Waterway, which is an equal stretch of inland water, and various inlets and channels. The station doesn't lack for jurisdiction.

During its early years, Wrightsville was covered by a Coast Guard station at Oak Island. But as Wrightsville grew and more emergency calls came in, Oak Island proved too distant. Obtaining a Wrightsville station, however, proved a decades-long chore. Generations took part in the effort. In

1924, Congressman Homer Lyon introduced a bill in Congress to bring about a station at Wrightsville. In 1929, the year after the Coast Guard helped with Trouble the whale, Senator Owen Simmons introduced another bill, which brought a Coast Guard commander to town to investigate the possibility of a station. In 1939, three Coast Guard officials came to Wilmington to investigate, with the support of Senators Robert R. Reynolds and Josiah W. Bailey and Congressman J. Bayard Clark.

By the 1940s, optimism was growing. In 1941, the Wrightsville Beach Board of Aldermen reached agreement on buying land at the extreme southwest corner of the beach on behalf of the federal government. Funds for a Wrightsville station were actually appropriated before World War II. The war, of course, shifted priorities. During the war, the Coast Guard was stationed at Wrightsville and ran horse patrols covering the beaches. It helped evacuate the beach during a 1944 hurricane.

A permanent U.S. Coast Guard station for Wrightsville did not arrive until 1958. Today's somewhat larger facility, shown here, replaced it in 1969.
PHOTOGRAPH BY VICKI McALLISTER

At war's end, the plan for a permanent station was revived. It was not until 1952, however, that a Coast Guard unit finally was established at Wrightsville, the picket boat CG-38-809 arriving for summer patrol duty. And it was not until 1957 that a contract was entered into with the Coast Guard for a permanent station. The city of Wrightsville Beach contributed land behind the town hall, and a tiny 16-by-24-foot station at 400 Waynick Boulevard opened on January 1, 1958.

The facility soon proved inadequate. In 1969, a larger one was built at the south end of the beach, facing Masonboro Inlet. The station was dedicated in August of that year. Though still small by Coast Guard standards, it remains in operation. The station has seen numerous changes over the years, including the construction of a pier to accommodate cutters and to give their crews a place for rest and relaxation between long patrols. Old housing in the rear of the station grounds was demolished, and a parking lot was added. The station now includes four staterooms, each able to house four to 10 people. It also has a galley, a recreational deck, a weight room, and other facilities.

Sesta admits he doesn't really run the station. That duty falls to Nick, an aging black Labrador found on Christmas Day 1993 by a Coast Guard reservist investigating a trash bag alongside Interstate 40. Inside was a four-week-old puppy with broken hips. He was taken to the Coast Guard station, named St. Nicholas, and nursed back to health. The puppy quickly was given the run of the place, and then some. His Coast Guard career, complete with honorary ranks, has had its ups and downs, though. He's been demoted twice— once for leaving the property and being picked up by the dogcatcher, and another time for relieving himself on a desk. But since 2003, Nick has held the rank of chief, putting him on more or less even footing with Sesta.

An aging Black Labrador, Nick, has the run of the station and even the honorary rank of Chief. Nick was a four-week-old puppy when he was found on Christmas Day 1993, in a trash bag alongside Interstate 40. His hips were broken. The puppy was brought to the station, named St. Nicholas, and nursed back to health.
PHOTOGRAPH BY
VICKI McALLISTER

Nick has a bed in the day room, but on this particular fall day, he has been lying in the entryway to the station. When the boats return, he slowly gets up and walks on out to the dock. One by one, the men greet him. Sesta says Nick used to jump in the channel for a swim. Nowadays, the aging Labrador chooses to walk into the water from the beach.

The Coast Guard lists Wrightsville's missions as search and rescue, maritime law enforcement, oversight of aids to navigation, environmental protection, safe-boating programs, and homeland security. The latter primarily involves providing escorts for what Sesta calls "high-interest vessels" as they navigate up the Cape Fear River. Sesta says he's allowed to say no more. The Coast Guard's website explains that vessels that make port calls at countries not in compliance with international law may be boarded at sea prior to entry, have their movements controlled by armed escorts, and be searched either at sea or at dock.

Much of the Wrightsville station's work, though, is taken up with boater safety and about 150 search-and-rescue missions each year, most during the summer months. Some

"S&R" missions turn out to be much ado about nothing. But fully a third are truly dangerous, Petty Office James Lewis says.

Sesta says most boat operators think they know what they're doing. Far fewer actually do. Lack of experience, coupled with alcohol, makes for most problems on the water. Though elsewhere the Coast Guard intercepts drug smugglers, there's little smuggling at Wrightsville; Sesta says the only drugs he encounters are small quantities for personal use. A larger problem, he says, is drinking. There is, he says, a lot of it. Alcohol is involved in 90 percent of fatalities on the seas. Lewis often asks boaters if they know the drinking laws. Nearly all say they do. Few actually do. Lewis explains that a blood-alcohol content of .08 percent or greater is illegal for a boat operator, as it is for automobile operators in many states. But the Coast Guard can step in and exercise a more subjective standard; a boarding officer can deem that an operator is intoxicated.

Lifesaving is more common than one may think, and it takes a variety of forms. Sesta says that Travis Dobbins, a boatswain's mate second class, likely saved a life in July 2006. A 40-year-old man was standing on the bow of his 23-foot boat to stow a dive ladder and anchor rope as the vessel moved through Banks Channel. It hit the wake of another boat, dumping him into the water. A friend couldn't reverse the boat's course in time, and the man passed underneath it. The propeller hit him in the head, cutting him so badly he would later need 58 stitches. Even worse, the propeller also sheared off his right leg at the knee. The Coast Guard met the boat at shore, and Dobbins quickly applied a tourniquet to the severed leg. He also treated the man for shock until he was airlifted to a hospital. The man recovered. His foot washed up on shore a week later.

Boating accidents are the usual calls, but even planes can

be involved. In the summer of 2006, a man bailed out of his experimental plane over the surf at Topsail Island. The plane broke apart, but the man survived. Some aren't as lucky. In August 2005, a man piloting an experimental aircraft capable of taking off and landing on water or land crashed into the ocean off Figure Eight Island. The 2 A.M. crash killed both the man and a woman passenger. They had met hours earlier in a nightclub.

The Coast Guard emphasizes safe boating and tries to maintain a presence on the waters. Ashley Sikes, an enlisted man, says when Coast Guard personnel board boats, it's often to perform routine safety checks. "We check life jackets, flares, fire extinguishers, everything." Lewis says boaters are generally fine with the inconvenience. "It's rare you get attitude out there," he says. "Everybody's glad to have us out here. They know we're concerned about their safety."

That isn't the only advantage to being in the Coast Guard at Wrightsville. "This is the best fishing on the island," Sikes says, gesturing toward the docks. "Right in between here." Flounder, trout, red drum, and baby grouper are all in abundance.

But the very best part? Sikes grins. "Free parking," he says without hesitation. "You can't beat free parking."

Petty office James Lewis and Senior Chief John Sesta say boat operators usually think they know what they're doing. Far fewer do.
PHOTOGRAPHY BY
VICKI McALLISTER

Chapter Nineteen

MODERN–DAY TREASURES

George Lapinsky moves slowly along the beach on a warm afternoon in January, passing between sun seekers while waving a metal detector back and forth before him, inches above the sand. The Garrett 2500 looks like a metal disk on the end of a pole; Lapinsky handles it the way others handle a weed whacker. Costing nearly $1,000, the Garrett 2500 is an investment, unearthing a multitude of metals.

There are treasures to be found at Wrightsville Beach, different treasures for different desires, and though few of them were buried by pirates, they keep the hunters coming back time and again.

Mostly, Lapinsky finds coins in the sand. The detector can search up to 12 inches deep with enough electronic exactitude to distinguish pennies from dimes. Even on a bad day, he finds some. "This is the slow time of year. Summertime, people drink," he says, laughing a little, "and they lose a lot of things." He has found as much as $11 in a day.

He does it for the exercise, though, and not the coins. Lapinsky worked 40 years for Corning in Upstate New York and moved to New Hanover County about 1996. He did not take up his beach walks until 2002, when he was 69. Now,

Small treasures are under the sands of Wrightsville Beach. George Lapinsky and his Garrett 2500 find a steady supply of coins.
PHOTOGRAPH BY VICKI McALLISTER

he drives the seven miles to Wrightsville three or four days a week and walks the beach for two or three hours, sometimes more. Sometimes, his wife joins him. Always, the Garrett 2500 does.

Occasionally, it uncovers jewelry. "I've found three wedding rings, two or three class rings, and lots of silver rings," he says. He even was able to return one Hoggard High School class ring, which had the owner's name inside. "It was the first name I picked out of the phone book," he says. The others, he just kept.

Zach Martin is in search of a much more transient kind of treasure: waves. He stands now in a parking lot, shielded by his car, slipping out of a wet suit. He lives in Greensboro and has been coming here to surf for four or five years. Wrightsville is closer than Carolina Beach, he says, and the waves are better than at Topsail Island.

Martin admits to not being an elite surfer. Those who hang out at the Sweetwater Surf Shop or the Surf City Surf Shop know more than he. He says he goes about 100 yards out and can ride a wave up to 10 or 15 yards.

There's a beach break near here, about where Lumina used to stand, and the waves are steeper than at other places, he says. One thing that makes Wrightsville Beach surfing good is that the waves face north. It all depends on direction, he says. Fellow surfers agree. Sixteen or 17 are surfing in a group. On a good day, he said, there are hundreds.

Surfing is year-round at Wrightsville Beach. The next wave will be as good as the last — or better.

PHOTOGRAPH BY VICKI McALLISTER

Patrick Carroll stands this morning on the deck of a large dive ship docked at the Bridge Tender Marina.

Carroll is a marine biologist and research associate for the aquaculture program in the Center for Marine Science at the University of North Carolina Wilmington. A Maryland boy who spent every available minute at Ocean City, he became a certified diver while attending college in the 1990s. He moved to Wilmington and began working on a dive boat in 2001. "I haven't thought about leaving," he says. "The diving is what keeps me here. I dive every weekend." It's more than just pleasure. Carroll researches shipwrecks, plowing through both centuries-old newspapers and the sunken ships themselves, even shooting underwater video, then posting his findings online at www.WilmingtonDiving.com. A book may be in the offing.

North Carolina's coast, down to and including Wrightsville Beach, has been dubbed "the Graveyard of the Atlantic." Hundreds of blockade runners, sailing vessels, small craft, and even German submarines have gone down in these waters.

Patrick Carroll is a marine biologist and research associate for the University of North Carolina Wilmington. But on weekends, he is a diver. His treasure is the sunken ships that lie in the offshore waters of the Atlantic.

PHOTOGRAPH BY
VICKI McALLISTER

The large dive ship belongs to Aquatic Safaris, which runs dive charters out of the Bridge Tender Marina. The Intracoastal Waterway lies beyond.

PHOTOGRAPH BY VICKI McALLISTER

On weekends, Carroll is a mate for Aquatic Safaris, which runs dive charters. He doesn't dive the Confederate blockade runners, much closer to shore, in part because they are sanded over. Visitors to those wrecks are more likely to be shore divers than boat divers, he says. The *Fanny and Jenny* is a popular dive, he says.

He dives offshore shipwrecks and sometimes artificial reefs. "North Carolina is a huge dive destination," Carroll says. "It's rated number one for shipwreck diving in the world." Among the wrecks are

> * The *Cassimir*, 42 miles offshore. In heavy fog in February 1942, the freighter *Lara* knifed into the tanker *Cassimir*, seeing it too late to alter course. Five crew members were lost.

* Two tankers torpedoed by German U-boats in March 1942, the *Esso Nashville* and the *John D. Gill*.
* The "rosin wreck," 40 miles from Masonboro Inlet. The rosin wreck was discovered decades ago, and its identity remains a mystery. "Recently, I've done some research and believe it to be the steamship *Runa*, a Norwegian freighter that sank in December 1923," Carroll says. The *Runa* sank in rough seas, 22 people dying. Carroll says historic Coast Guard cutter logs and information from the Norwegian Maritime Museum make the case that it is the *Runa*.
* The *Normannia*, 40 miles offshore. "This is one of the prettiest wrecks," Carroll says. The freighter went down in rough seas in January 1924, but the sinking was slow, and everyone escaped. The water in the area is clear blue, so divers can see the outline of the wreck. Tropical fish swim alongside.
* The USS *Peterhoff*, a Civil War wreck three miles offshore, off Fort Fisher. The *Peterhoff*—first a Russian ship, then a British vessel, then a blockade runner, and finally a United States ship—collided with a Union warship in March 1864 and sank.
* The "old dredge" wreck, 14 miles offshore. "This could be the *Playa*," Carroll says of a ship that had just been outfitted when it sank in 1931. It went down in rough seas while being towed.

Rough seas have always been dangerous for ships, and they are no less so for divers who hunt their wrecked remains. One diver lost his life at Frying Pan Shoals on Father's Day in 2005, Carroll says. He was in a group of three who got cut off from the boat. One of the others made it back to the ves-

The Trask Memorial Bridge leads on to Harbor Island from the mainland. The drawbridge opens hourly for private craft. It opens at will for government or commercial vessels.

PHOTOGRAPH BY
VICKI McALLISTER

sel and alerted the Coast Guard. A search was started. Eight hours later, the Coast Guard found one of the missing divers still alive. The other's body was never found. "We found his weight belt," Carroll says.

Most dives are less treacherous, but all are eventful.

Two days earlier, Carroll's run was out to the *City of Houston*, a favorite site for Wrightsville and Wilmington divers. The *City of Houston* lies 48 miles into the ocean from Masonboro Inlet, or 50 miles from the Bridge Tender Marina, sunk in the Atlantic south of the treacherous Frying Pan Shoals.

The *City of Houston*, a passenger steamship bound from New York to Galveston, Texas, made it only to the Carolina coast before it got caught in a walloping storm on October 23, 1878. "It was carrying 30 passengers and crew," Carroll says. "A big storm came up. It was probably a hurricane, but in 1878, they weren't called hurricanes." The ship went down, but not before a passing steamship picked up everyone aboard.

Lost, though, was the cargo—mostly household merchandise bound for the West. "There were a lot of toys and Christmas presents," Carroll says. "Porcelain dolls and porcelain dogs have been removed. And china, jewelry, some silver serving bowls. Even photographs." Carroll pulls out a book with a picture of one of the photographs recovered, a woman's formal portrait in an oval frame, its 1870s appearance made odder still by the cracks and lines now running through it.

The *City of Houston*, sunk in 90 feet of water, still gives up souvenirs it has preserved for all this time. "The other day, I picked up a glass shard, which had 'Liver' on it," Carroll says. The shard was too small to tell much more. An expert suggested it likely meant one of two things: either it came from a medicine bottle or the ship was carrying liver.

Either way, it was a small treasure.

Treasures are where you find them. These kayakers in the Banks Channel are among the many who revel in Wrightsville's waters.
PHOTOGRAPH BY VICKI McALLISTER

Chapter Twenty

LOOP AROUND THE PAST

"Everybody loves The Loop," says Town Manager Robert F. Simpson.

"Everybody loves The Loop," says planning and parks director Tony Wilson. "Everybody."

It is a statement of outrageous hyperbole—there's nothing that *everybody* loves—and yet it may be true. In Wrightsville Beach, only a couple of things get nearly unanimous endorsements. The beach, certainly. And The Loop.

The scenic, triangular 2.45-mile pedestrian path loops around most of Harbor Island. It runs just inside the main roads, U.S. 74 and U.S. 76, which spread out in a Y from the drawbridge entrance to Wrightsville. The path goes across one bridge onto the outer island, connects with the sidewalk of North Lumina Avenue, and comes back across the other bridge.

The beach is why most people come to Wrightsville. But except for events like the Holiday Flotilla, which draws 50,000 to see a lighted boat parade, The Loop is second most days. "It is a draw," Simpson says. "When I get to work at a quarter to seven, there are people who have been out here— and that's year-round." Every weekend, one organization or

"The Loop" is a scenic, triangular two-and-a-half-mile pedestrian path around most of the inner island. It is a favorite on Wrightsville Beach. Everybody loves The Loop.
PHOTOGRAPH BY VICKI McALLISTER

another uses it for an event, he says. "You name the cause, they have a 'Loop walk.'"

Valerie Locklear agrees. She is about to take off walking this warm, sunny afternoon. Her dog, Oakley, is alongside. "It's a large attraction, for walking and running," she says. Locklear moved from Virginia to work at a local college and is out here a couple times a week. "I walk it a lot. It's a perfect loop." She used to roller-blade it.

The two and a half miles take as little or as much time as one wants. Safe from most automobile traffic, a Loop walker can easily be overtaken by the scenery, the ocean breezes, and personal thoughts. Gems abound for the observant. Historic cottages line North Lumina Avenue. A pocket park lies off Greensboro Street. And natural marshlands, the tiny Harbor Way Gardens, and a large recreational park with tennis courts, athletic fields, and parking lots—used by some Loop walkers—lie off Causeway Drive on Harbor Island.

Other inside-The-Loop gems too often go unexamined. A pair of early-20th-century beach cottages lies off Salisbury Street. Many Loop walkers leave their cars there, though too few go inside the cottages.

One old beach home, the 1907 Moore Cottage, houses the Wrightsville Beach Museum of History, which was started by the Wrightsville Beach Preservation Society in 1996. Museum director Ryan Pierce says the cottage was donated by two couples—John and Jan Burgess and Jim and Jeanette Greiner. Jeanette's parents owned the Hanover Inn, which was across the street. Next door to the museum, the 1940s Howell Cottage houses the Wrightsville Beach Chamber of

The 1907 cottage that houses the Wrightsville Beach Museum of History and the 1940s cottage housing the Chamber of Commerce's information and visitors center stand side-by-side inside The Loop. The traditional beach-side cottages were saved from demolition for newer beach homes. They were moved to the Harbor Island site.

PHOTOGRAPH BY VICKI McALLISTER

Museum director Ryan Pierce easily rattles off dates and facts about The Big Fire, the railroad and electric street cars, the piers, the blockade runners, the Carolina Yacht Club, the Hanover Seaside Club, the old hotels, even David Brinkley.
PHOTOGRAPH BY
VICKI McALLISTER

Commerce's visitors center. It was moved here in 2004.

To enter the museum, visitors step across tracks from the turn-of-the-20th-century Ocean View Railroad. The front room includes a display wall on Lumina, as well as displays on beach cars and hotels. Photographs abound; long-departed buildings and people still live here. A framed, yellowed front page from the 1934 fire shouts, "DESTRUCTIVE FIRE RAKES WRIGHTSVILLE." Here, too, is a large-scale model of the entire beach in 1910, extending from Station One and the Oceanic Hotel down to Lumina. A miniature beach trolley runs the tracks.

Displays on the formation of the island and Hurricane Hazel greet visitors to a side room. The public television piece *Lumina: Remembering the Light* plays continuously on a TV set. "The museum's holdings include artifacts from Wrightsville Beach businesses, hotels, personal effects, pictures, postcards, and written and oral histories," Pierce says. Most items were donated. A few were bought with the museum's modest budget.

The cottage's kitchen and bathroom are kept as they

might have been a century ago. Early-20th-century bathing suits hang in the bathroom.

Pierce gives a tour, easily rattling off dates and facts about the Great Fire of 1934, the railroad and electric street-cars, the piers, the blockade runners, the Carolina Yacht Club, the Hanover Seaside Club, the old hotels, even David Brinkley. The Kitty Cottage was where the Summer Sands motel stands now, on Lumina Avenue. Lester Newell began working in 1936 in Station One, and took over in 1940. Once he built his larger store, it had a soda fountain, beach items, bait, and tourist items—"a lot like Redix is now," Pierce says. Newell sold in 1968, later going bankrupt. Wings bought the location in 1992.

And Lumina, of course. Pierce notes that it had a bowling alley and a shooting arcade and was a major stop for the Big Bands. In 1909, a cupola was incorporated. About 1916, the roof letters and flagpoles went up. "The movie gallery [in the surf] was taken out after talkies came out, in 1931. You couldn't hear them above the ocean," Pierce says.

The museum charges but a few dollars for admission. It seeks donations and sells books and DVDs. It once held an annual fundraising, memory-sharing event, the popular Lumina Daze. The event ended in 2005 after 12 years, though it may be revived in the future.

Outside, it is the 21st century again. The Loop is alive with walkers.

One couple, George and Denise, have only recently returned to The Loop following George's health problems. "We've been walking in the night," he says. They walk the entire route, Denise says, and then some: "We've even walked the beach." They drive down from Ogden just for the pathway. "This is very nice," George says. "I even have a shirt that says, 'I walked The Loop.'"

The Loop is now officially "The John Nesbitt Loop,"

One of the museum's main exhibits is the scale model of Wrightsville Beach circa 1910.
The display, of course, has to include Lumina.
PHOTOGRAPH BY VICKI McALLISTER

renamed for the late public-works director who oversaw
its construction. Nesbitt, director from 1979 to 1999, was
honored posthumously during a 2006 naming ceremony.
A sidewalk marker in front of the town hall credits him as
The Loop's creator. "I am so happy about it," his widow, Ann
Nesbitt, said at the ceremony as their sons Neal and Mark
watched. "He would have been thrilled."

Nesbitt oversaw the paving of The Loop bits and pieces
at a time, Simpson says. The pieces were not necessarily connected at first. It was, as Nesbitt joked, a road to nowhere.

By Nesbitt's own account, it took five or six years to
complete The Loop. "It wasn't all me," he said in 2001, as
quoted in *Wrightsville Beach Magazine*. "I had some folks in

public works that actually got real interested in it, and wanted to see it completed. It turned out a lot better than I ever thought it would. I never imagined it would turn out as well as it has. I never really did."

It could hardly have turned out better. The path is peopled by runners, walkers, bike riders, and stroller pushers. It is rarely empty.

"Summertime, it's packed," Valerie Locklear says as she heads off with Oakley, her dog-droppings bag in hand. "You'll have dogs, people riding bikes, runners. But it's never uncomfortable. There's a respect on The Loop. . . .

"I love The Loop."

Everybody does.

Chapter Twenty-One

WRIGHTSVILLE TOMORROW

Betty Bordeaux stands on the side porch, watching walkers go by, just as she might have done half a century ago. Or just as her great-aunt might have done nearly a century ago.

It is a comfortably warm Sunday morning, and the breeze is both warming to those who have just come outside and cooling to those who have been exerting themselves. It is like so much else on Wrightsville—all things to all people.

Nowadays, the island is a bustling resort in summer while still a turtle-slow retreat in winter. Large hotels dominate the sky, yet small, quaint period cottages hug the sands. But for how long? Multimillion-dollar rental properties go up alongside multigenerational homes at a rapid pace.

Bordeaux's is the latter. Her home on Lumina Avenue, now identified as the Williams-Bordeaux Cottage on a Wrightsville Beach historic landmark plaque, has been in her family since it was constructed about 1917. She remembers the stories. Her mother, Elizabeth Dock, later Elizabeth Dock Bordeaux, spent her teenage summers here. Her great-aunt, Lillian Williams Huggins, sold the cottage to Betty's father, William Bordeaux, in the 1940s. They were fortunate there even was a cottage to sell. The Great Fire of 1934 took virtually everything at what was then the north end of the island. It came roaring up the island to the house just south of the family home. It licked the side of that adjacent house. Suddenly, miraculously, the fire stopped and retreated where it came from. Six homes were spared.

Bordeaux's grandfather Alrich Dock owned an oyster restaurant on the edge of the mainland in the early decades of the 20th century, at the site of the present-day Bridge Tender Marina. "I have one of his business cards. 'All the oysters you can eat—50 cents,' " she says. His thriving business also had sheds for parking the cars of Wilmingtonians and other visitors. The visitors would then board one of the trains to the island while Alrich Dock kept watch over their automobiles.

Bordeaux was born in 1937 and grew up spending summers at the graceful shingled cottage with the wrap-around porch. "It certainly was a lot quieter," she says,

Betty Bordeaux leans down from the porch of the house she first saw when she was a child. "It certainly was a lot quieter," she says of Wrightsville Beach then, laughing at the understatement.
PHOTOGRAPH BY
VICKI McALLISTER

laughing at the understatement. In the late 1930s, this was the next-to-last house at the north end, Bordeaux says. The famous trolley line reached up here, but barely. To the south, the stations were numbered one through seven. There was only one unnumbered stop on this northern extension. The end of the line was just the other side of the next-door house.

The island had a different ambiance then. "Instead of a sidewalk, there was a boardwalk," she says. That meant a difference well beyond construction materials. When the town put in the wooden walk, it had to take three feet of the family's front porch. Even now, the boardwalk long gone, the truncated roofline attests to the porch shaving. But the boardwalk also was a money-making opportunity. "We went out with a stick and chewing gum on the end of it," Bordeaux says, smiling, "and reached down for nickels." It was a tried-and-true summer job for children at Wrightsville Beach.

When Bordeaux was about 10, her great-aunt—her grandfather's sister—was at the cottage. "When we bought the house," she adds, "we inherited my great-grandmother, who was in her 90s." With all this supervision, the children of the house had some rules. "We always had to get out of our bathing suits and into clothes for dinner and supper."

Lumina, of course, was the island's big attraction. "My mom loved dancing at Lumina," Bordeaux says. "They said it was the best dance floor on the East Coast." Bordeaux took dance classes at the pavilion but otherwise was uninvolved. She was away when Lumina was torn down and doesn't remember any attempts to save it. The preservation movement was not strong at the time, she says.

Bordeaux became a psychologist and moved to Goldsboro, North Carolina, in 1960 to start a career in the school system. She returned to Wrightsville in 1994 and has lived in

The Bordeaux-Williams Cottage has been in Bordeaux's family since it was built in 1917. It was one of only six to be spared by the Fire of 1934.

PHOTOGRAPH BY VICKI McALLISTER

the cottage since. Her family later bought the 1924 cottage next door.

Bordeaux admits to having thoughts of selling her cottage, which still maintains some of the original white cedar shingles as siding. She's considered it "many times," she says, "especially after Hurricane Fran. We lost half the roof."

But she hasn't sold and doesn't expect she will anytime soon. The cottage almost certainly would bring a windfall and even more certainly would be knocked down and replaced. She gestures across the street to a home built in 1934 that is still in the same family, and to a house behind it where the same is true, and to one next to it where the same is also true. In all, six homes in the area were here in the 1930s. They are still owned by the same families.

Bordeaux is chairman of the town's historic landmark commission. The commission bestows blue display plaques on homes reaching 50 years of age and especially coveted green plaques on homes that are deemed historic landmarks. Hers is one of about 20 Wrightsville homes that have landmark status—and the 50 percent tax break that goes with it. The historic landmark designation also comes with a preservation requirement: Anyone wanting to tear down a landmark home must wait a year before doing so.

It is a minimal requirement. Bordeaux laments the slow but sure disappearance of the Wrightsville Beach she has known. "I hate to see it go," she says. "But I understand. Money talks."

The past has never been far from the present in Wrightsville Beach.

But what about the future?

Oceanfront homes now sell for $1.5 million to $3 million, Town Manger Robert Simpson says. Even in the middle of the island, homes sell for $1 million. Tax bills have gone up exponentially. "The seasonal people are not bothered by the taxes," he says. After all, they had the money to buy million-dollar houses as second homes anyway. But "older people are being faced with the loss of their properties."

Beyond the vacationers and visitors, Simpson sees three groups with vested interests in the island: the old group, whose members want to hang onto as much of the old Wrightsville as possible; new, wealthier owners, who tend to buy property as second homes; and business people. Their interests are not always aligned.

Nearly all new structures are built on the sites of old ones that have been knocked down, Simpson says. Very little open land remains on the island now. "We're 90 percent built out," he says, before amending that. "We're more than 90 percent built out."

There are restrictions. The town has a 40-foot maximum building height, in recognition of ecology and aesthetics. Of course, that doesn't count the hotels and condos that went up before any limit. Even today, builders often apply for variances to go higher. The requests are shot down; 40 feet is high enough. That includes the required elevation off the ground, a necessity on a storm-battered island, which leaves room for parking under the living area. Most new homes or duplexes, then, have two stories of living area with high ceilings. Some squeeze in three levels.

Tony Wilson, director of planning and parks, says there's been a decrease in commercial projects as land values have risen. Some residents fear that small shops and restaurants may dry up on the island, replaced by expensive housing. Now being advanced, he says, are mixed-used projects with shops on the lowest floor and housing above. One thing helps: "Some commercial can be put on the bottom floor if it's flood-proof, in some areas." Otherwise, the bottom floor exists only to boost the others off the ground by eight to 10 feet, or 13 to 15 feet above mean sea level, under the 2006 flood ordinance.

One thing is certain. When old homes are sold, knocked down, and replaced, "they always build larger," Wilson says.

Peggy Gentry and her husband moved to Wrightsville Beach in 1954, moved away for years, then returned in 1988. "In the winter, when you drove on the beach, there were very few lights," she says of a half-century ago. The off-season island was practically deserted.

Growth in population, though, is not what stands out most. "The biggest change is in the homes," Gentry says. "Wrightsville Beach in the '50s and '60s used to be small cottages." Now, large homes and duplexes go up. Neighbors leave. The new owners are rarely year-round residents. They are more likely to have built a second home or rental property. Is the old Wrightsville Beach being lost? "Oh, yes," she says. "It's been gone. . . . At least the board [of aldermen] had the sense to keep the height of 40 feet. I fought hard for 35."

The Gentrys have a home built in 1988, next door to a four-apartment building from the 1950s that they also own. Assessments have gone up in staggering fashion. Would they sell? "No way," she says. "We've been offered and offered and offered. But we're not going anywhere."

The problem, of course, is too little of a good thing. Around 1970, Rupert Benson wrote, "It is comforting to say, while Wrightsville Beach has changed and improved greatly, it has not, to the present time, and will never be the 'honky-tonk' type, but continued to be that clean, refined and high

A few weeks earlier, a traditional beach cottage sat on this spot on Oxford Street. The house was bought and demolished, while a sign proclaimed what was "Coming Soon" ...
PHOTOGRAPH BY VICKI McALLISTER

type home-like resort for probably all time."

High-type homes, indeed. The new economics of the beach affect even vacationers, co-owner Allan Middleton of Roberts Market says. The old houses once rented for maybe $1,000 a week, he says. New ones are going for $5,000 to $7,000. Wilson thinks the town needs a parking deck to handle the staggering summer traffic. Or maybe shuttles from distant parking lots—beach trolley shuttles would be a nice touch.

It's hardly a situation unique to Wrightsville Beach. Baby boomers wanting coastal retirement living are causing "the Hilton Headization of the Coast," claims an environmental group, the North Carolina Coastal Federation. Its 2006 *State of the Coast Report* suggested six steps to saving what is left of the coast: (1) Getting serious about protecting the quality of coastal water; (2) Engaging in bottom-up land-use planning that involves residents; (3) Providing public and commercial

... What was coming turned out to be, no surprise, a modern beach house, much larger than its predecessor. That has been the pattern on Wrightsville in recent years.

PHOTOGRAPH BY VICKI McALLISTER

access to the waterfront; (4) Using government money to protect and even buy waterfront property; (5) Requiring a portion of new housing developments to be "affordable"; and (6) Providing tax relief to those who want to maintain their property rather than turn it over to developers as it skyrockets in value.

Bill Creasy grew up at Wrightsville Beach. "I was born in Wilmington. My parents had bought a home here in '26," he says, sitting in the kitchen of his small home on the backside of the island. "I was born in '28." Every summer from Memorial Day to Labor Day, the family lived in the beach home. Because school wasn't out yet in early June, Creasy had to ride the trolley from the beach to Wilmington for school every morning. "It was a lot of fun. I really enjoyed that." Another thing: "We called it a beach car. We never called it a streetcar. The front of the car said 'Beach.' "

Summers were glorious for Creasy and the other young boys of the beach. All of them had small boats and would play in the channel. "It was kind of a paradise during the summer."

Creasy went away to North Carolina State, took a job with the Atlantic Coastline Railroad, and was transferred to Georgia. He did a stint in the air force during the Korean War, then returned to the railroad in Georgia before retiring in 1986. He came home to Wrightsville. One of the island's foremost de facto historians, he has been instrumental in the development of the Wrightsville Beach Museum of History. Indeed, he even made a museum model of his old favorite, the beach car, along with one of a streetcar and one of the Little Chapel on the Boardwalk.

Changes to Wrightsville Beach were dramatic in the four

Bill Creasy lives in the third of his family's houses on Wrightsville Beach. The first two were taken by fire, one in 1934 and the other, on this spot, in 1976. The second fire killed his father. He apparently had gone back in to look for his wife, not realizing she was already out.

PHOTOGRAPH BY
VICKI McALLISTER

decades he was gone. They have been equally dramatic in the two decades since he returned. He watches as several homes are sometimes sold in a week, most to be knocked down and replaced by something built to the legal limit.

Still, he loves the town. "To me, it's special," he says. But he concedes that Wrightsville has "lost a lot of the allure that it used to have before getting so overdeveloped." Creasy once knew everyone he encountered. Those days are long gone.

He built his small two-story home—with one story of elevated living space—in 1978. It is his family's third home on the beach, built on the site of the second. Tragedy overtook the first two. The first, a few blocks from the current site, was bought in 1926 and lost in the Great Fire of 1934. The second also was lost in a fire, in 1976. That fire took his father's life. It started in the heat pump and soon overtook the house. "My dad went back upstairs to get something." Creasy thinks his father may have gone to get his wife, not knowing she was already out. "He was overcome by smoke. He didn't get out."

It's something else that threatens his house now. Growth

is taking over the island as inexorably as anything since the blaze of 1934. Once, Creasy's home was the middle of three about the same size. Now, his is dwarfed by those on either side, one built in 2004, the other in 2005.

The buildup, he knows, "is not going to change. It's a trend that's going to keep going." The skyrocketing property values are to blame. "It's not the houses. The houses are worth nothing. It's the land that's worth all the money." Elderly people on fixed incomes, whose families may have owned the homes for generations, have little choice but to sell. They can't pay the increased taxes. Some have been eager to get the windfall profits. But most never wanted the money. They wanted their family homes at the beach.

Creasy stops for a moment. He has been talking about the phenomenon as the plight of others. He knows he can't exclude himself.

Creasy's house once was in a row of modest cottages. On either side now, those cottages have been sold, razed, and replaced by large structures built to the legal limit.
PHOTOGRAPH BY VICKI McALLISTER

"I probably won't be able to stay here," he says softly, "because they're going to tax me out of it."

But is the glass half empty or still mostly full?

Within a generation or less, the only period cottages at Wrightsville Beach may be the museum and the welcome center, moved from the beach to Harbor Island.

"When I became executive director in April 2003, the museum was the fourth-oldest building remaining on the beach," Ryan Pierce says of the 1907 cottage. It is now the second-oldest, trailing only the French-Bluethenthal Cottage. The other two were torn down in favor of new beach homes, he says. The Broadfoot Cottage, built in the late 1800s, was replaced by family members with a modern home. The Solomon-Howe Cottage, constructed in 1900, was bought by a developer and replaced.

Pierce has devoted his career to preserving history. He is nonetheless philosophic. "On the one hand, it is sad to see these old cottages destroyed and lose their historic significance," he says. "On the other, if I invested $1 to $2 million on a lot that does not even consider the cottage in the appraisal value and cost because of its age and the understanding that it will most likely be demolished, I would want to maximize my investment as well."

Town Manager Simpson is likewise philosophic. He understands the burden on fixed-income homeowners, and he understands the nostalgia. He also understands the reality. "We have some people who would just as soon secede from the United States, raise the drawbridge, and never lower it again. . . . The reality is, you can't stop change."

Despite the changes, Wrightsville retains its allure. "It's

Wrightsville has changed constantly since development began in the 19th century. But the island maintains its allure. "Here's the beauty of Wrightsville Beach," one longtimer says. "Of course, it's changed. Of course the houses have gotten large and more elaborate. But the beach is the same. But the streets are the same." The feel of Wrightsville is unchanged.

PHOTOGRAPH BY VICKI McALLISTER

a great place to go. Everyone wants to go to the beach," Simpson says. "And then, historically, Wrightsville has been seen as a family-type beach, not a Myrtle Beach. So that allure is there."

As increasing numbers head to Wrightsville Beach, it's hard to argue that the allure is as strong as ever.

Allen Rippy is a car dealer and a lifelong Wilmingtonian and Wrightsvillian. He grew up in the '50s and '60s spending every summer day at the Carolina Yacht Club. He is not hurting financially—his dealership specializes in Cadillacs, Hummers, Saabs, and Saturns—but he talks of the glories of a Wrightsville Beach that money can't buy.

"It's the quaintness, it's the knowing everybody," he says, standing in Roberts Market with a few items he has picked up. "You know your policeman, you know the sanitation guy. It's the small, little community warmth that you don't see anywhere else."

For him, there's more. Rippy has surfed these waters since he was 13. Wrightsville, he says, has the best water on the East Coast until you reach Florida. "It has a consistent wave, just the way the beach is set up."

The Rippys sold their family home in the early 1990s but have another. He could easily live somewhere else. But why would he? "Here's the beauty of Wrightsville Beach. Of course, it's changed. Of course, the houses have gotten large and more elaborate. But the beach is the same. But the streets are the same."

The summer crowds can be difficult, he admits. "The Fourth of July is tough. You hunker down."

Despite it all, he believes Wrightsville has the same feel it has always had. "I definitely do. . . . I can't stop the change. You have to accept what you've been dealt. But if you look for it, you can still find it—Banks Channel, both inlets, Roberts Grocery right here, the Sweetwater Surf Shop, the Neptune. The Neptune's been here forever. I used to go in there when I was a boy."

The list is long.

Mornings are made for the beach.

On a chilly fall morning, the sun seems to come up slowly at Wrightsville Beach, at an island's pace. Scores of fishermen are already on the pier above. The beach is peopled by only a few predawn walkers. A couple in sweatshirts strolls by, holding coffee mugs brought from home. A woman has her camera ready. Nods and good-mornings are exchanged. A few more people arrive.

They are here to see the sunrise. Most may not be aware of the history or issues of the island. The Seashore, the Tarrymoore, Lumina. The railroad, the trolley line, the hated automobile. The Blockade Runner, the Holiday Inn, the Shell Island Resort. The jetties, the inlet closings, the beach nourishment. The first cottages, the modern-day duplexes. All were seen as progress. All changed the island.

The alliance is uneasy. In the end, nature seems to win more battles than it loses, accommodating man where it sees fit, fighting him elsewhere with hurricanes and nor'easters, beach migration, escarpments, and even fires.

But this morning, out here on the beach, nature is calling. The surf rolls in and out, in rhythm, in invitation. Sea gulls fly overhead. In its relative emptiness, the beach seems unchanged from the time the first builders showed up a century and a half ago. The sand is smooth, swept clean by the night's tide. A few prized shells have been left behind for the earliest on the beach.

The sun finally makes its appearance this fall morning, electrifying the ocean with oranges and blues. The beach walkers, most of them, stand looking outward. The caps of the waves are almost blinding in their whiteness.

Acknowledgments

Relatively few historical works have been written about Wrightsville Beach. There are photography books, both old and new, and Wilmington histories that mention Wrightsville in passing, but little more. Two compilations of historical notes do stand out, however: local historian Lewis Philip Hall's uneconomically titled *Land of the Golden River: Historical Events and Stories of Southeastern North Carolina and the Lower Cape Fear*, volume 1, *Old Times on the Seacoast, 1526–1970*; and Wrightsville Beach town clerk–treasurer Rupert Benson's *Historical Narrative 1841–1972 of Wrightsville Beach, North Carolina*, completed by his wife, Helen, after Benson's death. An index compiled by Wilmington's late researcher *extraordinaire*, Bill Reaves, makes Hall's volume more useful.

Two sources of information aid in the research of any locale: firsthand interviews and old newspaper accounts. However flawed the historical perspective, both give immediacy that can't be found elsewhere. Among the most helpful people I talked with were Bill Creasy, Betty Bordeaux, Roberts Market owners Jerry Allen and Allan Middleton, Allen Rippy, Peggy Gentry, and Wrightsville Beach town manager

Robert Simpson and planning director Tony Wilson. Others are named within these pages, and I hope that will suffice as an expression of my gratitude. Among newspapers, I'm particularly indebted to the *Wilmington Star-News* and its various predecessors, the old *Wilmington Messenger*, and the current-day Wrightsville newspaper, *Lumina*, and its sister publication, *Wrightsville Beach* magazine. For many of these, I am indebted to the aforementioned Bill Reaves, as is almost every other writer who puts together historical information from southeastern North Carolina. Reaves kept old newspapers from going to the scrap heap, then clipped and filed them in usable fashion.

I also owe a debt of gratitude to a number of professional researchers, most notably Beverly Tetterton of the North Carolina Room of the New Hanover County Public Library in Wilmington and members of her staff, including Joseph Sheppard; Ryan Pierce of the Wrightsville Beach Museum of History; Margaret Cotrufo of the North Carolina State Museum of Natural Sciences; and David Grabarek of the Library of Virginia, who helped me locate many an obscure North Carolina volume from a state away. My good friend Allan Libby of the Greater Topsail Area Chamber of Commerce and Tourism provided a number of contacts and bits of information I never would have found otherwise.

Graphics artist Roy Wilhelm of the *Richmond Times-Dispatch* has again crafted an attractive and useful map that merges the past and present.

The talented folks at John F. Blair, Publisher, have now published two of my books and I hope will not stop there. Carolyn Sakowski, the president, has brought together a group of writer-friendly people, starting with herself. Steve Kirk, my editor, makes all my words better and even seems to have developed a literary version of cinematic "speed ramping"—quickly getting past the boring stuff and into the good. Blair books are always beautiful, and Angela Harwood has crafted this one. Nobody does a better job in sales and marketing, respectively, than Ed Southern and Kim Byerly.

Bill Creasy helped read the manuscript, as did my three grown children, Lindsay Zarse, Ryan McAllister, and Jamie McAllister, all of whom are either teaching or headed that way, and whose backgrounds in history or English proved helpful. And I can't leave out my parents, Bob and Joan McAllister, who offered encouragement, as well as sleeping arrangements on our research trips to Wrightsville.

Finally, but foremost, of course, is my wife, Vicki. She has been the photographer and sounding board for both coastal books, and my best friend for far longer.

Bibliography

Much of the information in this book comes from the author's observations and interviews. Among the reference works consulted are the following:

Barnes, Jay, *North Carolina's Hurricane History*. 3rd ed. Chapel Hill: University of North Carolina Press, 2001.

Benson, Rupert L., and Helen S. Benson. *Historical Narrative 1841–1972 of Wrightsville Beach, North Carolina*. Wilmington, N.C.: Carolina Printing and Stamp Co., 1972.

Block, Susan Taylor. *Along the Cape Fear: Images of America*. Dover, N.H.: Arcadia Publishing, 1998.

———. *Cape Fear Beaches: Images of America*. Charleston, S.C.: Arcadia Publishing, 2000.

———. *Wilmington through the lens of Louis T. Moore*. Wilmington, N.C.: Lower Cape Fear Historical Society and New Hanover County Public Library, 2001.

Brimley, H. H. "Do What You Can *Now* With What You Have." *Museum News* (November 15, 1930): 8–12.

Brinkley, David. *11 Presidents, 4 Wars, 22 Political Conventions, 1 Moon Landing, 3 Assassinations, 2,000 Weeks of News and Other Stuff on Television and 18 Years of Growing Up in North Carolina.* New York: Alfred A. Knopf, 1995.

Fales, Robert Martin. *Wilmington Yesteryear.* Self-published, 1984.

Farb, Roderick M. *Shipwrecks: Diving the Graveyard of the Atlantic.* 2nd ed. Birmingham, Ala.: Menasha Ridge Press, 1995.

Gentile, Gary. *Shipwrecks of North Carolina: From Hatteras Inlet South.* Philadelphia: Gary Gentile Productions, 1992.

Gerdes, Susan Taylor, "Hurricane Hazel: An Ironic Anniversary." *Tidewater* (October 1984).

Hall, Lewis Philip. *Land of the Golden River: Historical Events and Stories of Southeastern North Carolina and the Lower Cape Fear.* Vol. 1, *Old Times on the Seacoast, 1526–1970.* Wilmington, N.C.: New Hanover County Public Library, 1981.

Harden, John. *The Devil's Tramping Ground and Other North Carolina Mystery Stories.* Chapel Hill: University of North Carolina Press, 1949.

Howell, Andrew J., Jr. *Money Island.* Wilmington, N.C.: Commercial Printing Co., 1908.

Hutteman, Ann Hewlett. *One Hundred Golden Summers: A History of the Hanover Seaside Club, 1898–1998.* Wilmington, N.C.: Wilmington Printing Co., 1998.

———. *Wilmington, North Carolina: Postcard History Series.* Charleston, S.C.: Arcadia Publishing, 2000.

Koeppel, Andrew. *Wilmington Then and Now.* Wilmington, N.C.: Andrew Koeppel, 1999.

Long, John D., Edward K. Rawson, and Charles W. Stewart. *Official Records of the Union and Confederate Navies in the War of the Rebellion.* Series 1, vol. 9, *North Atlantic Blockading Squadron, from May 5, 1863, to May 5, 1864.* Washington: Government Printing Office, 1899.

Martin, Margaret. *A Long Look at Nature: The North Carolina State Museum of Natural Sciences.* Chapel Hill: University of North Carolina Press, 2000.

McAllister, Ray. *Topsail Island: Mayberry by the Sea.* Winston-Salem, N.C.: John F. Blair, Publisher, 2006.

McCarl, Helen W., and Huw Christopher. *"What God Hath Wrought": A History of the Little Chapel on the Boardwalk, 1907–1992.* Wrightsville Beach, N.C.: Little Chapel on the Boardwalk, 1992.

Mitcham, Bill. "The Day the Whale Came Ashore." *The State* (November 23, 1963): 11–12.

Mohn, Celia. "Wrightsville Beach: Nature's Nightmare or Sunny Sanctuary?" History honors thesis, Duke University, 1984.

Old Trudge. "Nine Years After Hazel." *The State* (December 21, 1963): 8–10.

Perdew, Margaret "Peggy" Moore. Transcript of March 3, 2004, interview. Oral History Collection, William Madison Randall Library, University of North Carolina at Wilmington.

Reaves, William M. *"Strength Through Struggle": The Chronological and Historical Record of the African-American Community in Wilmington, North Carolina, 1865–1950.* Edited by Beverly Tetterton. Wilmington, N.C.: New Hanover County Public Library, 1998.

Sadler, W. J. "Wrightsville Nears Centennial." *The State* (May 12, 1951): 8–9.

Schoenbaum, Thomas J. *Islands, Capes, and Sounds: The North Carolina Coast.* Winston-Salem, N.C.: John F. Blair, Publisher, 1982.

Simpson, Bland. *The Inner Islands: A Carolinian's Sound Country Chronicle.* Chapel Hill: University of North Carolina Press, 2006.

Sprunt, James. *Derelicts: An account of ships lost at sea in general commerce and a brief history of blockade runners stranded along the North Carolina coast, 1861–1865.* 1920. Reprint, Southport, N.C.: Dram Tree Books, 2006.

Tetterton, Beverly. *Wilmington: Lost But Not Forgotten.* Wilmington, N.C.: Dram Tree Books, 2005.

Town of Wrightsville Beach Historic Landmark Commission.

Historic Walking Tours of Wrightsville Beach. Wrightsville
Beach, N.C.: 2000.

Walsh, Bill. "How Do You Spell Relief? W-R-I-G-H-T-S-V-I-L-
L-E." *Wrightsville Beach* (March 2007): 37–49.

Watkins, Greg, and the Wrightsville Beach Preservation Society. *Wrightsville Beach: A Pictorial History*. Wrightsville
Beach, N.C.: Wrightsville Beach Publishing Co., 1997.

Index